NOTES FROM OLD LYME

NOTES FROM OLD LYME

Life on the Marsh
& Other Essays

SYDNEY M. WILLIAMS

Bauhan Publishing
Peterborough · New Hampshire
2016

ISBN: 978-0-87233-212-6

Library of Congress Cataloging-in-Publication Data
Names: Williams, Sydney M. (Sydney Messer), 1941-
Title: Notes from Old Lyme : life on the marsh and other essays / Sydney
   M. Williams.
Description: Peterborough, New Hampshire : Bauhan Publishing, 2016.
Identifiers: LCCN 2015043713 | ISBN 9780872332126 (softcover/gatefold
: alkaline paper)
Subjects: LCSH: Williams, Sydney M. (Sydney Messer), 1941—Homes
and haunts—Connecticut—Old Lyme. | Old Lyme (Conn.)—Biography. |
Old Lyme (Conn.)—Social life and customs. | Country life—Connecticut—
Old Lyme. | Outdoor life—Connecticut—Old Lyme. | Williams, Sydney M.
(Sydney Messer), 1941—Travel. | Williams, Sydney M. (Sydney Messer), 1941—
Political and social views. | Williams, Sydney M. (Sydney Messer), 1941—
Philosophy. | Conduct of life.
Classification: LCC F104.O36 W45 2015 | DDC 974.6/5—dc23
LC record available at http://lccn.loc.gov/2015043713

Book design by Kirsty Anderson and Henry James.
Cover design by Henry James.
Photos from the collection of Sydney M. Williams III and by Sarah Bauhan,
except the following photos: on page 74: Duck River Cemetery, ©2014
Johanna Kaplan, used by permission; on page 84, on page 81, Veteran's
Memorial in Old Lyme, ©Town of Old Lyme used by permission; Inde-
pendence Hall Courtroom, Philadelphia, PA, ©2008 Aaron Vowels, Lou-
siville Kentucky, used by permission; page 90, Poppies Field in Flanders,
©2007 by Tijl Vercaemer, used by permission through Creative Commons
License.

BAUHAN
PUBLISHINGLLC
PO BOX 117 PETERBOROUGH NEW HAMPSHIRE 03458
603-567-4430
WWW.BAUHANPUBLISHING.COM

To Caroline, my wife,
with whom I have had a love affair
for over half a century

CONTENTS

LIST OF PAINTINGS

PREFACE

To inhabit the same world as mr. williams is a high privilege; to inhabit the same volume, even as doorkeeper, is perilous. Ogden Nash's Foreword to *Nothing but Wodehouse* begins similarly, though of course he wrote "Wodehouse," not "Williams." There is a connection: on a sunny Sunday afternoon in September of 1987, Sydney Williams telephoned to ask for my catalogue of Wodehouse first editions, English and American, thus inaugurating a friendship that has continued for almost thirty years. The furthest possible from being real drones, Sydney and his Wall Street cronies had formed The New York Drones (after Bertie Wooster's Drones Club in Dover Street, London); in 1991 some of them crashed a Wodehouse Society convention to hear me speak, an event still at the top of my list of many more modest achievements. Unlike the Hollywood starlets whom Wodehouse spoofs, Sydney is truly happy among his four thousand books—fifteen shelves comprising a fine Wodehouse collection.

It is not my place to tell you what to look for or what you will find in this volume, a marvelous mixture of memory and ever-present mindfulness, but I may be permitted to tell you a few of my favorite things. Sydney is smart, well-informed about finance and politics, as indeed I am not, and he writes so well that he makes them accessible to the likes of me. Better yet, the range of his reading impresses, even challenges, a retired schoolmaster who majored in classical languages and taught English for almost forty years. Apart from the essays themselves, which you may devour over breakfast, lunch, even dinner, are the rubrics— those nifty quotations heading each chapter, so called because a few hundred years ago they would be printed in red ink—ranging from Aristotle through FDR and John Steinbeck and Lady Bird Johnson to

Pete Seeger and Dr. Seuss, not to mention Edgar A. Guest. "Me, poor man, my library was dukedom large enough" says Shakespeare's Prospero, and I think Sydney might well say the same. The rubrics alone in this book could form a syllabus that I would proudly claim my own.

"Life on the Marsh." Sydney and Caroline more than once invited me to Old Lyme but upon my first arrival, as I pushed the bell-button, I dropped on their flagstones a large bottle of what I thought was a rather nice sherry. I mentioned that, but no one else did, and when I went out in the very early morning, it was gone. Silence be! It was the cat! I wandered up Smith Neck Road, and then toward the marshes and the mouth of the Connecticut River, which I had crossed up-river hundreds of times, in Springfield. Only in my imagination do I remember sheep, but I am pretty sure there were ducks, the railway striding over the arches near (as Dickens puts it). Like Jody Baxter in *The Yearling*, I felt a sense of loneliness that was not lonely: Caroline was by then in the kitchen, and soon Sydney and I would be looking at his Wodehouse books.

Allusive, illusive, occasionally elusive, Sydney has produced a book of essays which, in the words of Richard Brinsley Sheridan, it shall ever be my study to deserve. Read on here, happily, wisely, and well.

Charles E. Gould, Jr.
Kennebunkport
Christmas, 2015

INTRODUCTION

F OR THE PAST FIFTEEN YEARS, a variety of essays have appeared like magic on my computer at home. For lack of imagination, they were filed under the omnibus title "Notes from Old Lyme." They are also reflections, in the sense that they echo a slower, simpler way of life, away from our complex, continuous, electronically connected world. Today we spend most of our time in perpetual motion, generally responding to beeps and sounds from our BlackBerries, smartphones, and iPads. Physically, we are never still. It is easy to hop onto a bike or jump into a car or a taxi, and not much more difficult to board a bus, train, or plane. While each day has no more hours than the ones our grandparents knew, ours are consumed by more data, trips, demands, and communications than they could have imagined. As a result, we have less time to think, to consider, to reflect.

I often think of my maternal grandfather, who was responsible for the U.S. Rubber Company's far-flung rubber plantations. He would typically be gone for nine months, leaving by steamer for England, and from there going by way of the Suez Canal to Malaysia. He might return traveling east, across the Pacific, through the Panama Canal, and south to Brazil. Through those long trips he was not hounded by e-mails, nor did he record "selfies" to send back to his wife and children. It had to have been lonely, but he had time to reflect about himself, his family, and issues of the day.

Most of us would not like to live in that day, but I do envy the time he had to just think. These essays represent moments I have taken away from consuming life to, in fact, enjoy its small pleasures—at times alone, but most often with family and friends.

The oldest essay in this collection dates to September 13, 2001, two days after the treacherous and calamitous attack, the after effects of which continue to dominate our nation at home and abroad. It's titled "Thoughts on the Tragedies of September 11." The most recent, "Where Have All the Frogs Gone," concerns the process of aging—both sobering and inspiring when you consider how lucky we are to have been born.

In an attempt to provide some semblance of order to what is truly a medley, they have been divided into four loose groupings: "The Great Outdoors" deals with subjects as diverse as the marshes in front of our home and climbing Mount Washington with grandchildren. The second, "The World at Large," encompasses musings on 9/11, thoughts about Memorial and Veterans Days, and an essay on partisan politics. The third grouping, "Books and Other Interests," is the shortest, gathering thoughts on reading, laughter, and the violin. The final section is devoted to family and friends.

There is no hidden message in these essays. What you read is what you get. They were rewarding to write and, I hope, will be a pleasure to read. Other than a few grammatical corrections, the essays appear as they were written. While they are not in chronological order, the dates they were written have been provided because, in a few cases, they are relevant.

NOTES FROM OLD LYME

THE GREAT OUTDOORS

GROWING UP ON A SMALL FARM in Peterborough, New Hampshire, and now living on the marshes that front the Connecticut River in Old Lyme, Connecticut, I have always been deeply anchored in the outdoors. When I was a child, on winter weekends when we weren't skiing, my mother would admonish us, "Go outside and play." Reluctantly we would put on coats and mittens, and pull on our boots. Once outside, our imaginations allowed us to play games impossible inside: tramping through the woods, playing cowboys and Indians using stone walls as defensive positions, staging games of hide-and-seek, or just playing in the hayloft while listening to the animals below.

If one works in an office, as I did for almost fifty years, or spends time writing, as I do now, one is outside too little. Yet the outdoors retains its delight and its importance to our well-being. The essays in this section I hope will provide some sense of nature and the joy that being outside can bring.

The Return of the Bluebird

March 14, 2011

And the Spring arose on the garden fair,
Like the Spirit of Love felt everywhere;
And each flower and herb on Earth's dark breast
Rose from the dreams of its wintry nest.

"The Sensitive Plant," 1820
Percy Bysshe Shelley (1792–1822)

SATURDAY MORNING, LIKE MOST PEOPLE in the world, I awoke to the devastating news of an explosion at one of Japan's largest nuclear power plants, the Fukushima Daiichi facility in Okuma. The blowup was a consequence of the fifth-largest recorded earthquake in history and the subsequent tsunami that swept twenty-three-foot-high waves six miles inland. Cracks in the casing of the cement structure allowed radiated plumes to escape, potentially making this the worst nuclear power plant disaster since Chernobyl in 1986. (A no-go zone of twenty miles continues to surround Chernobyl twenty-five years after the accident.)

When not speaking of the devastation in Japan, reporters turned to the news of a 5:00 a.m. bus accident on I-95 in the Bronx. A tour bus returning to New York's Chinatown from Connecticut's Mohegan Sun casino overturned, killing fifteen and leaving five severely injured.

Trying to digest the meaning and to understand the randomness of these horrific events and the role chance plays in our lives, I began my morning exercises, standing on my Bosu warming up and looking out toward the marshes and the Connecticut River. Amazingly, the first thing I noticed was that our bluebird family had returned, a harbinger of spring. Later that morning, working in our flower garden, I saw that the season's first flowers—snowdrops—had pushed their way through

the warming, but still cold, soil. Ten thousand or more people may have died in Japan's earthquake and the ensuing tsunami, and fifteen died in the Bronx, allegedly a consequence of human error. Lives have been snuffed out, but life endures.

Man's capacity to overcome disaster has been shown time and again. The ability to do so does not diminish the awful nature of the calamity, but it is how the species survives. In 1888, in *Twilight of the Idols*, Friedrich Nietzsche wrote, "What does not kill me makes me stronger." Japan, in 1945, was destroyed. With a population of seventy-one million in 1940, the country lost an estimated three million people—4 percent of its population. Cities were bombed. Industry was destroyed, along with railroads, cargo ships, and port facilities. Yet twenty-three years later, in 1968, Japan had become the world's second-largest economy. In 1995, the Kobe earthquake killed more than six thousand people. In the aftermath of that quake, according to Peter Tasker writing in the *Financial Times*, more than a million Japanese, demonstrating man's humanity to man, volunteered their services.

In February 1945, on top of Mount Belvedere in Italy's Apennine Mountains and after a bloody fight attacking entrenched German mountain troops, my father wrote to my mother, not of the casualties or of the explosions of land mines, but of the buds of new flowers poking their way through the blood-drenched snow. The war in Europe still had two and a half months to go and thousands more would die, yet amidst all that death, budding flowers, those perennial symbols of renewal, were making their presence known. Death and destruction resulting from natural or man-made causes are, unfortunately, inevitable aspects of our lives; but so too are hardy flowers, budding trees, and the return of songbirds to our New England gardens heralding the renewal that this season brings. And so too are the fortitude and determination of mankind.

Knowing no one on the fated bus driving down from Mohegan Sun early Saturday morning and having no relationship to the ten thousand Japanese killed the same day, it is easy for me to look through those calamities to the morning that will surely come. But we have all experienced tragedy and we know that the passage of time, while never fully healing the wounds, makes them bearable. That bluebird, sitting atop his red birdhouse last Saturday morning, was a sign that days of renewal lie ahead.

An Afternoon on the Golf Course
July 24, 2003

While playing golf today I hit two good balls. I stepped on a rake.

Henny Youngman (1906–1998)

O N THE FOURTH OF JULY I birdied the seventh hole at the Old Lyme Country Club. Lest anyone confuse me with Tiger Woods, let me take you through the first six holes of that round.

The opening hole is a 330-yard par four. My initial drive carried the ball two hundred yards and into the rough about ten yards off the fairway. Lying about 130 yards from the pin with water about eighty-five yards away, I selected a seven wood. I flubbed the shot; it sailed low, hit the water, skipped twice with God-given grace, and ended in some weeds twenty yards from the green. An easy chip shot turned into a monster. The ball flew high and came down fifteen yards on the far side of the green. A deliberate calm, enhanced by a frustrating tension, allowed me to chip the ball onto the green. Three putts and I holed out in seven.

The second hole starts off over water and, lying alongside and to the right of the first hole, it ascends the same hill down which I had just come. The hole is 370 yards to the pin and is ranked number one in terms of difficulty. Using my new $480 driver, I looped the ball about 120 yards, just carrying the water and landing slightly off the fairway in the rough on the right. Shots number two and three advanced the ball about 100 yards into the rough on the left side. A miraculous five iron carried the ball 130 yards just shy of the green. So, lying four, I chipped the ball onto the green. Two putts and I recorded my second triple bogey.

Three is a tricky par three. It is only 112 yards to the pin, but it is virtually straight downhill. Sand traps border the hole. A small, paved road that incidentally is magnetically attractive to golf balls runs to the left of the green. On the right lie bulrushes, water, and some bullfrogs.

An eight iron carried the ball into the bulrushes. A dropped ball was pitched into the sand. My third shot (fourth if one allows for the drop, but who's counting?) put me on the green. Two putts and the ball was in the cup in five (or six).

To get to the fourth hole one must hike, or ride, about 150 yards up the previously mentioned road to a noncontiguous piece of property comprising fifty acres, on which lie holes four, five and six. The fourth hole is an "easy" par four with a dogleg to the right. The distance from the tee to the pin is 304 yards. The angle can be cut, and the distance shortened, with a well-placed two-hundred-yard drive that carries either over or through some trees. Generally, it is not difficult to get on the green in two. My drive started out as planned, but the ball, on the way to the fairway, met a tree. I heard the *clop* of ball meeting tree, but never found the former. Being fair, but not stupid, I dropped a ball in the light rough just off the right side of the fairway with an open shot to the green. An eight iron moved the ball about thirty yards; my pitching wedge then found the green. Two putts and I was home. This time I included the dropped ball and marked a six on my scorecard.

Hole five is a short par four whose topography must be described to be believed. The hole is 298 yards to the pin with a slight dogleg to the left. From the tee a hill slopes steeply down into a gully, then sharply up. The two-hundred-yard marker lies about fifteen yards from the crest. From the top of the hill one looks down on the green, but in between lie trees and an igneous outcropping covered in dense brush. The green itself is positioned on a small mesa within a hollow. My opening drive carried the ball just over the brow of the hill, and it looked like the ball would end up just left of what little fairway there is at that spot. I never found its landing place; so I put down another. With my pitching wedge, I shanked the ball farther into the brush. This time the it was dropped just off the green and was chipped on. Two putts allowed me to hole out in seven.

The next hole—six—is the longest of this nine-hole course. It is 467 yards to the pin along a hilly but pretty straight course. My opening drive carried me just past the red tees—about eighty yards out. Two seven woods and a seven iron finally brought me within pitching distance of the green. Even a duffer is allowed one good shot per hole, and my wedge from 110 yards out arced beautifully and got me on the green in five. Three putts later and I was home in eight.

The trek to hole seven takes one back along the same road taken to four. The tee at seven sits across the small pond that threatens the green on hole three. The pond, as mentioned earlier, is home to a number of bullfrogs who have a habit of croaking in the midst of one's downswing. The course goes across the little pond and up a slope so steep that carts are not allowed. The drop from the crest is about thirty yards to the green. The distance from the tee to the pin is 165 yards. Selecting a five iron, like a blind man in a dark room I marched to the tee. A slow and deliberate backswing followed by a perfect swing, and the ball sailed true. I saw it drop just over the crest. It rolled to within eight feet of the pin. Grabbing my clubs, heart palpitating, I headed for the green. Taking my time, and after careful study of the position of the ball relative to the pin, I approached the ball with controlled trepidation. In my long career I could count on both hands the number of holes I had parred. Now I had an opportunity for a birdie. Nobody was around to make me nervous. (Of course, nobody was around to confirm my story either.) I gripped the club, then remembered to relax. I picked a spot to aim at, drew the club back slowly, and let it drop gently. The ball rolled true and with a *plink* dropped into the cup. Birdie!

Elated, but with no false sense of expectation that I could repeat the performance, I picked up my clubs and headed for the clubhouse.

An Early Morning Row
September 28, 2003

"Nice? It's the only thing," said the Water Rat solemnly,
as he leant forward for his stroke.

The Wind in the Willows, 1908
Kenneth Grahame

THE AIR IS COOL AND CLEAN. Under my feet the grass is still wet with the morning dew, as I walk the three hundred yards from my house to the dock carrying oars in one hand and my scull's seat in the other.

The best time to row is early in the morning when the water is quiet and the only people on the river are early fishermen and crabbers. Mist rises from the water as the cool morning air comes in contact with the water still warm from the late summer sun. The dock reaches out into the Duck River, a marsh creek that connects the Lieutenant River to the Back River. In turn these two rivers flow into the Connecticut about two miles and one mile, respectively, from Long Island Sound.

As I walk toward the water, the sheep look up from their breakfast grazing. I acknowledge their look. Seagulls flit about overhead. Osprey nests are now largely empty, their occupants having retreated to warmer climates. Crows call out with their high-pitched, short screams of irritation. I cross a catwalk and then a narrow mowed field

to where my scull rests upon its rack. Lifting the boat, I rest it easily on my head—the twenty-seven-foot length belying its thirty-eight pounds. At the beam the scull is eighteen inches, but its outriggers provide an overall width of six and a half feet. I carry the scull across the second catwalk to the small dock, which, being low in the water, is perfect for launching an equally low-in-the-water boat. Having placed the seat in its tracks, I gingerly grasp the oars in my right hand (freeing the left to hold on to the dock should the need arise), place my right foot in front of the seat, and carefully set myself down.

Sitting backward in a narrow scull, precarious in its balance, provides an interesting and all too familiar perspective from which to view the world. (Wall Street, where I work, is, like most businesses, best understood when viewed with knowledge of its history.) The past is what faces me. To see the future I must awkwardly turn my head and shoulders, carefully, so as not to upset the boat. As I edge away from the dock I take quarter-strokes, which gradually lengthen as I move into the current of the river until I'm at a point where I'm sliding forward. My knees come up to greet my chin, at which point the blades of the oars dig into the water, allowing me to pull on the oars while simultaneously pushing back with my legs. The boat spurts forward—or backward, to the oarsman. I move upstream with the incoming tide, but against the current. Rowing across Duck Pond, I enter a canal that connects to the Lieutenant River. The Lieutenant is notable, at four and a half miles in length, for being Connecticut's shortest river. The headwaters are a marsh area fed by a stream called Mill Brook and

made famous by naturalist and birder Roger Tory Peterson, whose home was on its western edge.

The beauty of the environment is exceptional. The salt marshes and the creeks that drain them are filled with cattails, sedge, black grass, and the ubiquitous phragmites. Muskrats, raccoons, and even mink make their homes in the banks of the river. Overhead—besides seagulls and ospreys—ducks, cormorants, plovers, marsh wrens, and swallows dip and dive. It is little wonder that the Nature Conservancy has declared the tidal basin of the Connecticut River one of forty Last Great Places in the Western Hemisphere.

My focus, alas, is on staying upright and powering the scull forward. But as the tempo smooths and I begin to relax, a state of quiet ecstasy embraces me. The work is monotonous in its repetition, but the delicacy of the balance keeps me alert. It is at this point that I feel a sense of oneness of man with boat. Sliding forward, I feather the blades backward across the water until the catch is reached, at which point the blades are given a quarter turn and dropped into the water; I then push off with my legs while simultaneously pulling on the oars to the point of release when the blades are again raised, given a quarter turn, and feathered back. The process is repeated. The silence of the moment is interrupted only by the calling of birds and the splash of water against the gunwales. My course takes me up the Lieutenant, under a railroad bridge, under Route 156, and then under I-95. I row past the village of Old Lyme with its picturesque homes, past the Florence Griswold Museum where Connecticut impressionists were painting a hundred years ago, until I reach a point where the river widens before disappearing into the marsh; turning around, I row home.

An hour after leaving the dock I return whence I came, this time watching what had been the future recede into the past. The rising sun has warmed the air and swept away the morning mist. Walking back to the house, glad to be again facing forward, I feel a satisfaction brought about by intense exercise while communing with the natural world that surrounds me.

Life on the Marsh
September 29, 2009

*Poets who know no better rhapsodize about the peace
of nature, but a well-populated marsh is a cacophony.*

Bern Keating (1915–2004)
Writer and photographer

ACROSS THE CONNECTICUT RIVER from our house, clearly visible with binoculars, is the sign identifying the Old Saybrook restaurant Dock and Dine. Directly in front of us, on the tidal flats of the Duck River, we have our own Fly in and Feast. Seagulls, egrets, and herons on spindly legs, eyes sharp and beaks at the ready, walk delicately across the mud looking for mollusks and invertebrates, newly revealed by the ebb tide.

A saltwater marsh is abundant in life and abounds in the sustenance necessary for its inhabitants. It is an eat-or-be-eaten world. Fiddler and blue crabs, snacking on smaller creatures, sidle through the muck, wary lest they become breakfast for a hungry gull. This symbiotic life is ever-present. Muskrats slither from their embankment homes hoping to snag a fish—a fish that escaped being supper for an osprey the evening before.

The name of the river is derived from the Algonquin word *quinnetukut*, which means a long, tidal river. It rises just above the Moose Head flowage on the New Hampshire–Canada border. It starts as not much more than a stream. At its Long Island estuary, 407 miles south, it separates Old Lyme from Old Saybrook by two miles. The river serves as a migratory corridor for Canada geese, great horned owls, American black ducks, mallards, great blue herons, and great white egrets, among others. As winter descends and the northern reaches of the river ice over, American bald eagles can be sighted as far south as Old Lyme. In the spring, as the earth warms, ospreys return to fledge

their young, nesting on natural and man-made platforms.

According to science writer Beva Nall-Langdon, brackish tidal marsh productivity can approach that of most high-yielding crop-lands—up to ten tons per acre per year, though three to six tons is more common. Mr. Nall-Langdon writes: "This abundant biomass decays each year, resulting in large quantities of detritus." This detritus provides a food source for creatures from mollusks and fish to much of birdlife.

A recent study of Ragged Rock Creek in Old Saybrook identified 115 different plant species. Marsh rivers are abundant with seaweeds, such as *Cladophora* (mermaid's hair), which can entrap one's oars when rowing, and sea lettuce, both of which are fitted with air bladders allowing them to float on the surface. On land, but within the tidal plain, can be found sedge, cordgrass, eelgrass, cattails, goldenrod, and bulrushes. These grasses serve as both food and nesting material for birdlife. The ubiquitous and nonnative phragmites, which has been degrading the marsh for several years, has been attacked in recent years by the Department of Energy and Environmental Protection under a marsh restoration program, and is now in retreat. These grasses grow six to eight feet in height, cutting off the light and destroying native grasses. Their disappearance is welcome.

Animal life on the marsh is omnipresent. Mollusks, including blue mussels and eastern oysters, can be found on the river floor, and provide food to birds, as well as to crustaceans including fiddler and blue crabs, horseshoe crabs, and shrimp.

Besides marine fish such as porgies, flounder, and blackfish, the river is home to anadromous fish, such as Atlantic salmon, American shad, American eels, and striped bass. In all, the Connecticut River is home to about sixty varieties of fish. During late fall salmon return to their natal waters, often traveling hundreds of miles upstream to the freshwater where they were spawned, climbing man-made ladders to avoid man-constructed dams.

The return of the salmon after years of absence is testament to the work done by the United States Fish and Wildlife Service, the DEEP, and the Nature Conservancy. In *A Statistical Account of Middlesex County*, published in 1819, the author wrote (regarding the Connecticut River), "For several years the quantity of fish in the river has very considerably decreased." Raw sewage, tanneries, and a lead mine were all partly responsible. The Industrial Revolution was in its infancy. People were more concerned with increasing their incomes than with environmental causes. As wealth came, attitudes changed, fortunately for those of us who now live along the river.

The marsh is home to a number of mammals and amphibians, including shrews, voles, frogs, turtles, toads, snakes, muskrats, and fisher cats. On occasion we have caught sight of weasels, which, while common in Washington, are rarely seen in our marsh. On the other hand, deer are frequent visitors, especially in the early morning, feasting on salt hay.

But it is the birdlife that is most readily apparent. As one walks across catwalks and marsh toward the water, red-winged blackbirds, marsh wrens, and swamp sparrows dart back and forth. Plovers and sandpipers patrol the mudflats, intermingling with seagulls and egrets in their search for morsels newly revealed on the glistening flats. Incoming tides bring diving birds, among them black ducks, cormorants, and mallards. Stately swans, while not native to the area and in fact considered a nuisance by the DEEP, sail gracefully with the current.

A saltwater marsh is dynamic. The salinity of the water changes with the tide, but more importantly with the seasons. Plant and animal life must adapt. Given the number of species of both classes, a remarkable balance has been achieved.

Bern Keating is right. Nature, defined as the material world existing without man, is neither tranquil nor peaceful. The sounds from the marsh, especially in the evening and early morning, can be discordant—eerie and beautiful at the same time, like an orchestra warming up. One life often depends upon taking another. A kill is executed not for pleasure, but to sustain life. Animals are territorial. Birds, with an uncanny homing instinct, migrate with the seasons from thousands of miles away to the nests they vacated months earlier. Should another bird have moved in, a fight ensues. Crows are particularly territorial and familial, and are quick and harsh in their call, to reclaim captured territory. Mammals live and die within a few miles, or less, of where they were born; the relocation of crustaceans, mollusks, and invertebrates depends upon tides and currents.

While the marsh is an important aspect to my life in Old Lyme, I find that environmentalists can be overzealous about their causes. A recent example was the subject of an article in Monday's *Investor's Business Daily*, pitting drought-stricken farmers in California's San Joaquin Valley against the delta smelt, a fish threatened under the Endangered Species Act. Water, a valuable commodity most places but particularly in this farming region of California, is being diverted into the ocean to save this smelt. As a result, according to some, 145,000 acres are creating a dust bowl equal to those of the 1930s. Unemployment in farming towns like Mendota has reached forty percent. Despite the pleasure the delta smelt provides to those who dine on it, life will go on without it. Every year thousands of species (including plants) disappear. New species appear or are discovered. The planet and everything on it is in constant flux. Common sense suggests that protecting a particular species must be weighed against the cost of its preservation. While the symbiosis and interdependency of life is a fact, no one species, including man, serves as the critical linchpin.

But back to my marsh: it reminds me of what New York's Lower East Side must have been like a hundred years ago—the sounds and the color; immigrants speaking multiple languages, practicing their own special religions, exhibiting their own customs, and wearing the clothing of their native lands. Though the marsh is not the melting pot that constitutes America, there is a symbiosis that is beautiful in the way it all works. Gazing from my window onto the tidal flats of the Duck River, I am witness at a peephole on life—a vision of a city in the marsh.

Kayaking on the Marsh Creeks
October 4, 2010

A river is more than an amenity, it is a treasure.

Oliver Wendell Holmes, Jr. (1841–1935)

If there is magic on this planet, it is contained in water.

Loren Eiseley (1907–1977)

ON WEEKENDS, LOOKING OUT at the Duck River, I see kayakers, at times in packs of a half dozen, other times alone. Some are obviously beginners, others old pros. They are young and old, men and women. They have in common a love of the marsh, a wish to be with nature, a desire for the outdoors and exercise, and a sense of serenity. Like Odysseus hearing the Sirens, but with no worries that I would be smashed on the rocks, I am lured toward the water.

For almost twenty years I have been sculling along the broader reaches of these marsh creeks. However, in sculling from my floating dock I must accede to the tides, as the dock at low tide is mired in mudflats, and to the early mornings, for that is when the water is still, or nearly so. As a form of exercise, rowing, unlike kayaking, is almost Zen-like, using all muscle groups, requiring intense concentration and a focus on position and on each stroke—especially the moment when one has rolled forward and feathered the oars back, readying for the "catch." A miscalculation can cause a rower to "catch a crab," sending him tumbling into the water, an occurrence that has been my fate more than once.

Ten years ago my children gave me a kayak. I bought a second to keep it company, for kayaking, unlike sculling, can be a social pastime. And it is possible to go out anytime, as long as the tide is in. Kayaks are small and maneuverable, allowing me to follow small creeks that con-

nect the larger ones. On a warm late-summer day I find myself alone on the water, marveling at the luck that has brought me to this place where we have a home, about two miles north of the mouth of the Connecticut River. In 1997, the entire Connecticut River was designated by President Clinton as one of America's Heritage Rivers. More recently, the river's estuary and tidal lands were listed by the Ramsar Convention on Wetlands as one of 1,759 wetlands of international importance—and one of only fifteen in the United States.

Other than kayakers, what one encounters most often are crabbers, men and women drifting in small boats, their engines idling as they drag up their traps laden, or so they hope, with fiddler, hermit, or blue crabs. Their activity is pleasant and comforting to witness. It is an ancient rite, stretching back to the earliest settlers and to the Indians who preceded them.

In my kayak, I paddle silently, slipping past a pair of male double-crested cormorants, wings extended in intimidation, while their lady friends sit nearby. I approach an eastern mud turtle, sunning himself (or herself?) on a log. As well, the sun warms my back. My double-bladed paddle moves slowly in a graceful arc, as quietly as possible. Water striders skim jerkily across the surface of slow-moving creeks, searching for even smaller insects on which to dine. Unlike a scull, a kayak allows one to "smell the roses," to let the mind wander, to think creatively. In this interlude with nature, New York and the turmoil of Wall Street seem distant.

My grandchildren enjoy a kayak outing. With one of my children, we take two of the little ones, making sure they are wearing bathing suits and life vests, and walk to the river. They are small enough that a grandchild fits on each lap. Paddling is a little less free, as arms must extend in front of the children. While wary at first, the children soon love being in the kayaks and out on the water. Unaware of the need to maintain balance, however, they twist and turn their bodies, shouting across the water at one another, urging their paddlers to go faster—turning our meandering voyage into a race. But it is delightful to be with them, as they listen to seagulls and watch ducks diving for dinner.

Once again, returning alone to the water it is easy to follow small marsh creeks and sense that one is alone in the universe, or that time has stepped back three hundred years. Sitting low in a kayak with marsh grasses at eye level and the only sound being the splash of one's paddle, the call of a seagull, or the whisper of the breeze as it softly pulls back the saltwater cordgrass, one can imagine what it might have been like for the first explorer.

While I love the company of others, and especially that of my family, in truth I am addicted to being alone, to silence and the proximity of nature when I am on the water.

Skiing in Vail

December 24, 2003

I'm still having fun and as long as skiing is enjoyable,
I'm going to continue to do it.

Bode Miller (1977–)

THE FLIGHT TO DENVER WAS FULL, as were my expectations. Sixty-five inches of snow had fallen in Vail since the first of November, and the mountain had been open for twelve days. According to the Vail website, 24 percent of the mountain, represented by nineteen lifts and 1,300 acres, was available to skiers.

Nine years earlier, in 1994, five of our current group of seven signed up for Pepi's Wedel Weeks. Pepi Gramshammer, a seventy-six-year-old former member of the Austrian Olympic ski team, began the program in 1985. It is designed for accomplished skiers who love the sport. Skiers of like ability are placed in small groups of five or six and are assigned an instructor from the Vail Ski School.

This, then, was our group: Bud Mantz and John Dominis met as young men in Dallas in 1952. Bud was in the process of building what would become a successful graphic design business, while John was a photographer with *LIFE* magazine. John's credits would later include a tour in Vietnam with the French prior to their defeat at Dien Bien Phu; he would accompany President Nixon to China, and he was the only photographer allowed in the inner circle at the Olympic Games in Mexico City in 1968. Bud and John have been friends for more than fifty years and have often skied together in the United States and in Europe. Helen and Bill Gilbert live in St. Louis and, since 1978, have had a condo in Vail. Bill runs a successful business with facilities in St. Louis and Wisconsin. Helen is an accomplished horsewoman who competes in hunter classes.

A good friend, Ned Hamarat, who had attended a Wedel Week the previous year, suggested I might enjoy it. So, December 1994 found the two of us in Vail signing up for Pepi's Wedel Week. Ned ended up in a class a level above mine, along with Bill Gilbert. I was put in a small group that included Helen, Bud, John, and one other. Assigned to instruct us was Lyle Viers, then fifty-five, a native Californian from Bishop. Lyle first appeared in Vail as an instructor in 1967. He then spent a few years coaching national junior women's teams and returned to Vail in the early 1970s.

As we all, tentatively, greeted one another that morning nine years ago, we had no idea of the friendships that would be formed. However, we soon glimpsed that ineffable something that would bond us together. Getting off the Vista Bahn chair at Mid-Vail on the first trip up, Bud Mantz's first question was, "Where are we going to have lunch?" Helen and I looked at each other and started to laugh. This was going to be fun. We knew we were soul mates. Any differences in our respective skiing abilities would take second seat to the camaraderie we felt. In 1996, during our third season, Hank Sykes joined our group. Hank and I are close friends and were first introduced through our wives who had both, reluctantly, attended a student-wives tea at the University of New Hampshire in September 1964. We were both completing our senior year at the time. Hank had been denied his diploma at Princeton due to the snippety attitude of the dean when Hank was late turning in his thesis. I—but that is a story for another time.

Pepi's Wedel Weeks were fun, but proved too confining for our free spirits. After four years of Wedel Weeks, we grew restless. We had a lot of fun together and we all loved to ski, but we felt that dispensing with fashion shows and mandatory lunches and dinners would be more fun. So December 1998 found us in Vail on our own. We were able to elude the grasp of Pepi, but Lyle stuck to us like wet snow on the bottom of a ski. (Actually, we had to prevail upon Lyle, who had been working with us diligently but fruitlessly, to abandon Pepi's Wedel

Weeks and come with us.) Two years later, in December 2000, Dene Hunt, a friend of Helen's, joined our group. Dene is an Australian who, because of her love of skiing, spends the winter months in Avon, a few miles from Vail village. Our group was now complete—Helen and Bill, John and Bud, and Hank, Dene, Lyle, and myself. (My friend Ned later joined us, as did another friend and his fiancée—Walter Harrison and Ann Howard.)

~❖~

Chair number four, which rises from Mid-Vail to Vail peak, emerges from the shadows to brilliant sun as it climbs out of a gully to the upper slopes a few hundred yards from the peak. At 11,250 feet, the air is thin and still cold, and my heart is racing in anticipation of the first run of the season. The morning sun and the distant vistas of the Gore Range provide a wholly unnecessary lift to one's spirits. The first run of the season on the new Stockli Laser 168s that I have rented is only moments away.

The skis glide easily. We follow in Lyle's tracks, Indian fashion. An inch or two of snow fell overnight on the groomed packed powder on Swingsville—a smooth, wide, cruising slope, perfect for the first run of the season. As I push off, the only sound is the whistling of the wind as my body attempts to respond to memories from last year. I try, not always with success, to keep my upper body stable, with arms and hands forward, and let the shaped skis carry me through sweeping S turns. Lyle stops about five hundred yards down the trail for the morning ritual of stretching. A few minutes later (and after a few sardonic witticisms—funny only unto ourselves), we continue down the hill. By the third run of the day we feel warm, limber, and comfortable. Initial feelings of apprehension have been put to rest, while muscles that have been at rest reemerge. A feeling of warmth and confidence spreads through the body, and the skis and the legs become as one. "It is better than sex," says one of us, without really meaning it. Skis and boots are nothing more than extensions of one's legs and feet. Ski poles, on the other hand, like the tail on a bobcat, run the risk of evolving out of existence. When successful, a skier becomes a study in rhythm.

Each day we get a little better. In spite of our attitudes and abilities, some of Lyle's teachings actually sink in. One day follows another. As our skiing improves, our confidence soars. We race down a groomed Riva Ridge, through the moguls on Power Glade and Showboat, with Lyle calling out, "Get more extension . . . get up on your edges . . . get your feet farther apart . . ." At 11:00 a.m. we break for hot chocolate, good conversation, and some gentle ribbing. A late lunch is preferred and the place of choice is the Game Creek Club. Lunch is a prolonged affair and the body seems a little stiff (pardoning the pun) after the wine and rich food. As we go outside and step into our skis, the midafternoon sun is unable to dispel the day's chill. Shadows are lengthening. We carefully pick our way down to the Game Creek chair, which carries us, cold and uncomfortable, to the top of Wildwood, from which we will descend to the village of Vail. However, after a few minutes our bodies are again warmed by the exercise, and the wine and the food coursing through our bodies act as a relaxant. We cruise through the trees on Owl's Roost, down over the steps on Ledges, and finally down Bear Tree, doing our best to let the skis do the work while we enjoy the ride. We arrive in the village in plenty of time for a shower and a rest before the next big adventure—dinner. On this particular night Liz and Luc Meyer of Left Bank have prepared for us a superb dinner, starting with a fresh lobster appetizer, followed by a perfectly cooked rack of Colorado lamb, and finished with a dessert consisting of a light and tasty cheesecake. After an aperitif or two, good and appropriate wines with the dinner, and lively and joyous conversation, we are ready for bed and for visions of tomorrow's skiing that will dance through our heads.

Were my expectations fulfilled? You bet they were, and more. To an easterner, the skiing was glorious. A westerner might have lamented that the back bowls were not open and that, for the most part, we were skiing on packed—not fresh—powder. I have been skiing a long time.

I received my first pair of skis fifty-nine years ago when I was three years old. However, I am there for the fun. It is not the number of runs or the speed achieved that is of consequence. It is, rather, the individual challenge, the beauty of the place, the joy of being alive, healthy, and outdoors, and the camaraderie of old friends that make skiing important to my life. Fifty-one weeks will pass before the eight of us will again be together. But it is the recall of those days—the morning sun on the snow-covered trees, fresh tracks through new powder, laughter rippling from underneath helmets and from behind goggles, and the cry of "Oh! Mona" resonating in our memory—that is the carrot that will bring us back to Vail next December.

Skiing the Bolshoi Ballroom
January 25, 2010

Skiing is a dance, and the mountain always leads.

Author unknown

About six inches of new snow fell overnight. We awake expecting Blue Ox to have been groomed, as that is the usual pattern in Vail. For those of us who love to ski but in whom age has reduced the flexibility and the stamina we once had, the groomed double-black-diamond Blue Ox, covered in fresh powder, presents a thrilling venue.

However, on closer examination of the grooming report, we realize that Bolshoi Ballroom in Siberia Bowl has also been groomed. It takes time to get there. One has to ride the chair out of China Bowl, glide along a catwalk about half a mile to what is known as Siberia, and then straddle a Poma lift to the top of ledges that form the bowl's northern perimeter.

When we reach the top, at 11,455 feet, with snow flurries competing with the sun, the view is breathtaking. Unmarked powder leading down through clumps of evergreens, which cling to the slope, gives promise of the ride to come.

My good friends Helen and Bill Gilbert of St. Louis and Walter Harrison of New York and I jump onto the slope, the lightness of the fresh snow providing little resilience against our turns while its softness makes silence an eerie but delightful companion—a silence only interrupted by sudden whoops of joy as we dance down the appropriately named slope.

It is difficult to explain to one not initiated in bowl skiing the thrill one gets as the skis pick up speed, the ease and the grace of the turns as one descends through fresh powder covering a groomed base—especially doing this on a slope where we are, for all we can see, alone. We slip between trees and bounce down the undulating slope, each turn providing a sense of freedom and elation. Drugs or alcohol could never provide the high one experiences in those moments of wild abandon when the only care is the anticipation of the next turn.

In a matter of moments we reach the bottom, the thrill gone as quickly as it arrived; we catch our breath and follow Silk Road back to the Orient Express; as the chair ascends, we look at one another. We do it again.

Thirty-One Hours on Mount Washington
August 20, 2007

This is the second-greatest show on earth.

Attributed to P. T. Barnum (1810–1891),
as he stood atop the old observation tower on Mount Washington

Behind dark-towering granite
The western sun sinks red;
And evening's silver planet
Mounts guard in Heaven instead.

"Mountain Sunset," *Granite Ledges*, 1943
William Plumer Fowler (1900–1993)

THIRTY-FOUR YEARS AGO I took my then six-year-old son, Sydney, on a hike in the White Mountains. Each summer for eleven years, into the early 1980s, we would spend a few days in the White Mountains. We climbed thirty of the forty peaks over four thousand feet, staying at huts manned by student employees of the Appalachian Mountain Club. A few weeks ago, accompanied by my now forty-year-old son, I took his son, Alex, aged six, on a similar hike. Mount Washington and the White Mountains have long held a sense of nostalgia for me. I grew up in Peterborough, in the southern part of the state, surrounded by what Henry David Thoreau refers to in Walden as the "Peterboro hills," Monadnock being the largest. When I was in my very early teens, my father took me to Mount Washington to ski Tuckerman Ravine. We stayed at Pinkham Notch Lodge, which was then operated by Joe Dodge.

New Hampshire has long stood for freedom and patriotism. Her license plate reads "Live Free or Die." Martin Luther King, in his 1963 "I Have a Dream" speech, proclaimed, "From the prodigious hilltops of New Hampshire, let freedom ring." Philip Carrigain, leading an expedition in 1820, named a number of the White Mountain peaks after presidents—northeast of Mount Washington lie Jefferson, Adams, and Madison. Mount Monroe lies just to the southwest. More recent presidents also have namesake peaks. For example, west of Monroe is Mount Eisenhower.

Compared to mountains around the world, Mount Washington at 6,288 feet is relatively small. But its modest height is deceptive. In 1932 the National Weather Service established the Mount Washington Observatory. As the highest in the Northeast, Washington's peak is subject to unusual wind currents. Its summit holds the record for the strongest wind ever recorded—231 miles per hour on April 12, 1939. Every three days, on average, hurricane winds sweep across its peak. Eleven years ago, almost to the day we made our way to the top recently, the wind was measured at 154 miles per hour, a record for the month of July. Sixty percent of the time the peak is enshrouded in dense fog, and the temperature averages 26.5 degrees Fahrenheit. The coldest temperature ever recorded on Mount Washington was minus 44 degrees Fahrenheit (with a wind chill of minus 103). More people have died on Washington (150 since 1849) than on any other mountain in the world except Everest, more than half from hypothermia. Reasons for the large number of deaths include its easy access by a large population and the fact that many people climb without proper equipment.

Sunday, July 22, proved warm and sunny. We left Pinkham Notch at 8:00 a.m., having had dinner the night before with an eighty-two-year-old physicist, Ben, from Princeton, New Jersey, who regularly climbs in the region. As a teenager in Czechoslovakia, he had been rescued by a British humanitarian group, which evacuated him and about a thousand other young Jewish people to England in 1938. We marveled at his life, and felt sobered by the good fortune we had to be born in this country.

The first two and a half miles follow the trail skiers use to get to Tuckerman Ravine. It is wide, rocky, and not terribly steep. About halfway up we pass Ben, who has decided he will climb to Tuckerman, but probably not go to the top. We wish him well and continue, arriving a little before 10:00 a.m. at Hermit Lake shelter. This shelter, at the base of the ravine, appears to have replaced the old lean-to, ironically called "Howard Johnson's" by generations of young skiers. Looking up toward Tuckerman from the shelter, we are awed by the sight of what lies ahead: Lion Head to our right and Boott Spur to the left, down which we will descend in the morning. Dead ahead are the steep cliffs of Tuckerman Ravine. It looks like half a teacup—getting increasingly steep as it approaches the rim.

We follow a narrow trail into and up the ravine, ascending through some trees that soon become scrub. The trail steepens as we break above the tree line, and we pass a lone patch of snow braving the July sun—the last bit of snow on Mount Washington. An early autumn might bring the beginnings of a new glacier, but it is unlikely that the snow will last through the dog days of August. It hasn't in the past one hundred years or so and it isn't likely that this year will be any different. The final part of the climb, up the rim, is hand over hand, but we arrive before noon and the view makes the effort worthwhile. Looking back, east across the ravine, we get a panoramic view of the Wildcat ski area—another trail that, accompanied by my father, I skied in pre-lift days.

Once over the rim, we are less than a mile from the summit. The trail leads across the Bigelow Lawn, a rocky area that brings to mind the story of Jabez Stone of Cross Corners, New Hampshire, memorialized by Stephen Vincent Benét in "The Devil and Daniel Webster": "If stones cropped up in his neighbor's field, boulders boiled up in his." For the average-size person, clambering over them is tiring but doable. However, for Alex, aged six, they represent a daunting challenge. But he makes it, and around 1:00 p.m. we arrive, completing the four and a half miles in five hours. The top of Washington is unlike any other peak in the White Mountains. We are greeted by cars (the road predates the automobile) and by the cog railway, which was built in 1869. There is a snack bar, a weather station, and the Tip-Top House, built in 1853 as a hotel and now a museum. The day is comfortable (temperature in the high thirties) with little wind, and after an hour or so we descend the

Crawford Path a mile and a half to the Lakes of the Clouds Hut, built in 1915 and operated since by the AMC (Appalachian Mountain Club). The hut nestles between Washington and Monroe, and we reach it in plenty of time to select our bunks, unpack, relax, and get to know some of our fellow hikers, including another eighty-two-year-old from Maine.

Following a communal supper prepared and served family-style by the college-age "croo," the sun gradually sinks into the western sky. The weather cools noticeably as night creeps up the western slope. Bunks beckon, and soon only the snores of hikers interrupt the stillness of slumbering mountains.

After breakfast, Sydney takes Alex up Mount Monroe—a half mile to the summit, giving him his second "White Mountain-over-4,000-footer." By nine we're heading down. The Camel Trail, marked by cairns (piles of rocks), leads to the Davis Trail, which gradually descends a broad shoulder of Washington toward Boott Spur, with Tuckerman Ravine another mile to our left. This is one of the starkest and most beautiful places in the White Mountains, and one is almost overcome with the sheer immensity of space and the barren, rock-strewn land-scape. There is an overwhelming sense of being alone in the universe. Boott Spur Trail goes off to the left, down a steep pitch. Beneath a darkening sky we descend toward the tree line. Once there, the trail, narrow and steep, drops another two seemingly endless miles until it finally intersects with the Tuckerman Trail a few hundred yards above Pinkham Notch. The skies, which have been threatening all morning, finally open up as we reach the car.

Thirty-one hours after we left, the lodge comes in sight; and, while I do not feel exactly like Anchises, I sense the passage of years and understand how the burden of Aeneas might one day descend upon my son. Indians native to the state knew Mount Washington as Agi-ocochook, home of the Great Spirit. As we pull out of the parking lot, taking a last look toward its cloud-covered peak, the name seems fit-ting. We view the mountain with respect. It draws hikers as a magnet does metal shavings. We, too, will climb it again.

A Hike on Mount Tam
November 2003

In every walk with nature, one receives more than he seeks.

John Muir (1838–1914)

T HE PATH SLOPES UPWARD AND AWAY from the paved road at a ten- to fifteen-degree angle. Almost immediately the air becomes cleaner, a good thing for those of us who, as the rise becomes steeper, inhale more deeply and breathe more quickly. Within a few minutes the view from the rock-strewn path provides vistas south toward San Francisco. The sky is blue, and the sun warms the late October day.

Today's hike began half a mile back when the seven of us, plus three dogs, gathered for lunch at Left Bank in Larkspur, which is in Marin County, California. Five—John, Lang, Lori, Jeff, and Garrison—live in the area and often hike in these hills surrounding and abutting Mount Tamalpais (more commonly known as Mount Tam), which stands in 6,300 acres of protected land and rises 2,571 feet. I join the group three or four times a year. The seventh is my son, whom I feel particularly fortunate to have along, as he lives with his wife and two children in London, but happens to be in San Francisco on a working vacation.

Having my son with us reminds me of his first hike, in the summer of 1972, in New Hampshire's White Mountains. That day three of us headed out early from Pinkham Notch (my younger brother, Willard, was with us). We started out enthusiastic and full of joyful expectation on a cool, drizzly August day. Seven hours later we arrived, wet and cold, at our destination, Madison Hut, looking a little like Aeneas carrying his father, Anchises, while leading his son, little Ascanius, by the hand out of Troy. On this day in California, though, the fates and good planning will provide a more pleasant hike.

We follow the trail up through open meadows, which appear some-

what barren to an easterner but are awesome in their vastness, with spectacular views of Mill Valley and the Bay Area. The cool air and the warm Pacific water create banks of fog that pass, ghostlike, through the Golden Gate Bridge and into San Francisco Bay. We stop, look back, and note that we are above the fog bank, and the office towers of the city sparkle in the sunlight. We are fortunate, we say, to be alive and able to enjoy this place of such beauty. The view also encompasses the prison at San Quentin and Alcatraz Island, serving as a sober reminder of the fragility, and the great rewards, of freedom.

The trail, which ascends a shoulder of Mount Tam, continues upward, dipping in and out of a wooded area before beginning its descent. Heading down, the steeply angled path follows a largely dry streambed. It will, I am assured, become a torrent in a couple of months when the rainy season is in full sway. Even now roots and rocks, smoothed by years of hikers' boots and eons of rainy seasons, are slippery. Long arms and strong hands become valuable appendages as we come down the trail. The dogs show approval of the downward, and homeward, journey in running ahead, then scrambling back, all the while looking for any damp place in which to cool their haunches. Zoë, John's Boston terrier, is particularly happy to be coming down. At six she is the oldest of the dogs, and with ten-inch legs she is certainly the shortest. (About midway up the climb I caught her surreptitiously giving John a glance that seemed to ask, "Why am I here?") Maggie, Jeff's puppy, is the youngest, most curious, and most energetic of any of us—dogs or humans. She is, I believe, a combination of pointer and Lab. She views us all as slow and dull. Lang's dog, Bennie, has the heaviest coat and so is the most interested in looking for a place to cool off. His look seems to say, "Hey, man, cool it. What's your hurry?" Bennie is the result of an unlikely meeting between a Newfoundland and a springer spaniel.

About two hours after setting out, we return by another road. A half-mile walk takes us past cars, people, and other signs of civilization—things that for a brief time we had shunted from our minds as they had been shut out from our vision. A refreshing and welcoming beer at the Lark Creek Inn puts a fitting finish to a short, but highly enjoyable, afternoon. We had been a band of brothers and a sister. Hiking up the trail away from houses and paved roads, we had a taste of what it must have been like for the first settlers. We sensed the vastness of our country with its richness and its beauty. With weary legs stretched before us, we feel blessed and thankful.

The First Storm of the Winter in New York
December 27, 2010

When I no longer thrill to the first snow of the season,
I'll know I'm growing old.

Lady Bird Johnson (1912–2007)

NEW YORK IS ALWAYS BEAUTIFUL during the first snowstorm of the year. As the winter drags on, a yearning for spring replaces the exhilaration of those first December flakes. But today, cars are absent, or at least cars in motion are absent. Those left on the street are barely visible beneath a combination of new-fallen snow and snow-plowed banks. And there are always a few cars left stuck in the roads by foolhardy souls who felt their Chevy sedans were impervious to snow. People are friendly. Everybody is in a good mood and says good morning, even those charged with shoveling the sidewalks. These are special moments in New York, unfortunately impossible to bottle and resell in late February when we tire of the thought of another storm, or during the sweltering dog days of August when anger percolates, for no visible reason.

Of course the next day, the white banks have become gray, slush has turned to ice, and tempers have reverted to their New York norms. However, this morning I walked over to Lexington Avenue, found one news store open, and proceeded to walk down the center of Lexington, then over to Third Avenue on Fifty-Fourth Street, past Citigroup Center, knowing the sidewalk would be shoveled. Third was busier and the sidewalks were generally clear; however, the spirit of freshness and renewal, so timely as we close out the old year, was palpable.

Restaurants were the same—nearly empty, but staffed with friendly waiters. A big storm infuses people with a sense of a shared experience, bringing them closer together, providing a fleeting glance at what a world without war and deprivation might really be like.

The sky this afternoon is blue; the sun is shining. The storm has disappeared, having moved off toward the north and east. Though it is cold outside, the clear sky reminds me of the innocent look Dennis the Menace would provide his neighbor following one of his diabolical escapades: Who, me? Likewise the Gulf of Mexico, just a few days after Hurricane Katrina, was as calm as a toad in the sun.

New York will always be exciting. It doesn't take a storm to enliven the place. It is a big city whose diversity makes it unique. That will never, I hope, change. On the other hand, this morning for a few moments—a few hours, perhaps a day—the city and its people were as one. We survived the big snow. We had experienced it together. Central Park recorded twenty inches, but with wind gusts up to 60 miles per hour, drifts were even higher.

A big storm is a way for nature to alert us as to who is in charge. Growing up in New Hampshire, I once thought that New Yorkers made too much of snowstorms. They didn't take them in stride. But having lived part-time in the city for fifteen years, I like the way New Yorkers handle the experience. So what if a taxi driver who grew up in Jamaica and has only been in the country for a few months has trouble driving in snow? It is to be expected. Who cares? This is where I now live and work, and there are few experiences more rewarding than seeing the city in the midst, and in the immediate aftermath, of an early snowstorm.

Where Have All the Frogs Gone?

May 27, 2015

> *Where have all the flowers gone?*
> *Long time passing.*
>
> "Where Have All the Flowers Gone?" 1955
> Pete Seeger (1919–2014)

EVERY SPRING MORNING, once the swimming pool has been opened, I clean the filters. Inevitably there are one or two frogs who wandered into the pool during the night. This is common after a night's rain lured them on a nocturnal stroll looking for snackable insects. The temptation of cold clear water causes them to hop in. Unfortunately, finding no easy way out, they lose strength and get pulled by the currents into the filters. By the time I get there, most have drowned.

This year there have been no frogs. Not being a herpetologist, or even much of a naturalist, I could think of no reasons other than the cold winter with its heavy blanket of snow, or some fungus that had become rampant. In search of an explanation, I read and contacted some experts. Frogs are amphibious, meaning they can live both on land and in water. The cold winter should not have affected them, as frogs are ectothermic, meaning they rely on the environment to regulate their body temperatures. They also survive long periods without eating. In the winter, frogs find a cozy place known as a hibernaculum that protects them from extreme temperature changes, as well as from predators. Only when its resting spot warms above freezing the frog's body thaws. It awakens, ready to eat and to mate.

The male emerges harrumphing, uttering mating calls, a sound with which those of us who live in the country are familiar. For the female that responds, her burden—after a few moments of delight—has just begun. She typically lays around 10,000 eggs, making my mother, who raised nine children, look like a piker. She lays such a large number because the odds on survival in this Darwinian world are small. (I wonder if my mother had similar thoughts?) Within a few weeks, the eggs that survive become tadpoles. In two to three months, tadpoles become small frogs. Life expectancy varies by species, but generally is six to eight years.

Writing about frogs got me reflecting on the extraordinariness of nature and the interdependency of all species. Frogs, for example, are pretty far down the food chain. Like most people, I marvel at and seek to understand what I understand least. Ospreys, one of nature's most beautiful birds, have returned in abundance to the marshlands at the mouth of the Connecticut River. Dr. Paul Spitzer, a naturalist who grew up in this area, explained that their return is due to menhaden, which have resurged. The menhaden is a foraging fish often used as fertilizer or crab and lobster bait by humans, but found especially tasty by ospreys. In this "knee-bone connected to the leg-bone" world of nature, the menhaden's return is due to plankton, which grows in abundance in our creeks, and to the fear of bluefish, striped bass, and other predators that inhabit Long Island Sound. The osprey's real name, for even those who are not interested, is *Pandion haliaetus*, which derives from Pandion, a mythical king of Athens, and *haliaetus*, Greek for *sea eagle*. To watch them soar and then dive, talons poised for a fish having no idea that its life is about to end, is a beautiful sight to see—except, of course, for the fish. No matter, the osprey is worthy of such a distinguished name.

While osprey feast on fish, their feathered friends the seagulls and hawks have been known to toss down a frog or two. So frogs, when not drowning in my pool, play a critical link in the food chain among shorebirds in our marshes. Typically, frogs eat insects, ridding us of natural pests. Having no teeth, they swallow whole whatever they have engorged. In turn, they themselves are also eaten by foxes (one of whom lives under our hedge) and swallowed whole by various snakes that slither about.

Living at the mouth of the Connecticut River is an extraordinary blessing. The marsh and the creeks that abut it, with the river and the sound a short swim or kayak ride away, are abundant with life. The estuary is one of the Western Hemisphere's forty Last Great Places, so proclaimed by the Nature Conservancy.

But to return to my concern about frogs: there are, from what I have learned, eleven species living in Connecticut. Among those that have found their way into my pool and its filters have been wood frogs, pickerels, and bullfrogs, but most common are green frogs, or so I believe from looking at pictures in the *Field Guide to Reptiles and Amphibians* by Roger Conant.

Like the flowers that Pete Seeger wrote and sang about, frogs die, as do all living things. Not only the individual, but also, over varying periods of time, the species. "The history of life," wrote evolutionary ecologist James P. Collins in 2004, "is a story of extinction: ninety-nine percent of the species that ever existed are now extinct." Regardless of what actions we may take, the same fate ultimately will be mankind's. We do what we can to survive—we try to limit our impact—but eventually nature wins. Its forces exceed anything man has devised.

In the meantime, however, I was happy to hear from Gregory Watkins-Colwell, collections manager for herpetology and ichthyology at the Yale Peabody Museum of Natural History. In response to my question about the absence of frogs in my pool, he told me that the cold winter had delayed their regeneration and mating. He added that a dry spring meant fewer nocturnal wanderings. He assured me they would show up. Wait, he said, for a morning after a good night of soaking rain. It hasn't rained, but I remain vigilant and hopeful.

Osprey
July 14, 2015

Within the slightest moment's breath,
Two mighty wings released,
Two claws full-stretched, two legs reach out
The sinews, strained, unleashed.

"The Osprey," 2008
Steve Hagget

N ATURE IS FILLED WITH WONDER: the changing of the seasons; the lifecycles of plants and animals; the symbiotic way in which all life coexists. I am in awe when considering that from single-celled, microscopic bits have emerged millions of different forms of life. The osprey, with its fierce yellow eyes, graceful flight, and sharp talons, is one of nature's most beautiful creations.

They are not uncommon, though the pesticide DDT and the Coast Guard's then policy of removing osprey nests from channel markers came close to killing them off in the 1950s and 1960s. The banning of DDT in 1972 and a change in Coast Guard policies permitted their survival. The recent return of menhaden has allowed them to thrive, at least in our part of Connecticut—the tidal marshes that compose the estuary where the Connecticut River meets Long Island Sound. From my dock I count twenty-two nests; most are located on Great Island, a marsh island that separates the Back River from the Connecticut. A nest was recently erected on the marsh in front of our house; another is in a large tree three hundred yards to the north.

Ospreys, like hawks and eagles, are raptors—birds of prey. The word *raptor* derives from the Latin word *rapere*, meaning "to seize or take by force." In ornithology, birds of prey have four character-istics: excellent vision; strong, curved talons for catching and killing fish; strong legs for holding what they have caught as they return to

the nest; and a strong, curved beak for tearing flesh. The osprey is unique among raptors in that its two outer toes are reversible. It is sometimes known as a sea hawk, as it is the only raptor that dines exclusively on fish.

Ospreys can reach two feet in length, with a six-foot wingspan, and weigh three to four pounds. They soar high above the water. When a fish is spotted, the osprey dives at high speed, hitting the water feet first, often fully submerging to bring up its catch. Its barbed pads allow it to hold its victim, which it then carries back aerodynamically, the head leading. The female is heavier than the male, with stockier legs. She guards the nest, her mass providing coverage for unhatched eggs and newly hatched young. The smaller male is better suited to be the hunter, diving for fish, eluding seagulls, and carrying his catch back to the nest.

Nests are built high to avoid predators like raccoons. In our area, they are usually built on man-made platforms. The bed typically consists of sticks, sod, and grasses. Ospreys tend to mate for life and have one brood a year. Eggs, of which there are generally two to four, are hatched in sequence, usually three to five days apart. In times of food shortages, the weakest will be sacrificed for the strongest, usually the firstborn. Chicks fledge in eight weeks—around the beginning of August—but it takes about three years for them to reach maturity. Life expectancy is anywhere from ten to twenty years.

Ospreys' migratory habits are, as with all birds, fascinating. Alan Poole, author of the 1989 book *Ospreys*, wrote of their migration from Martha's Vineyard. He strapped .75-ounce solar-powered satellite transmitters to the backs of a few. Cuba and Hispaniola (the island containing Haiti and the Dominican Republic) were the preferred destination of most, though some stopped in the Florida Everglades and others flew on as far as South America. One female flew the 2,700 miles from the Vineyard to the rain-forest rivers in French Guiana in thirteen days. The trip included layovers in Maryland, North Carolina, and the Bahamas.

The name *osprey* first appeared around 1460, according to researchers at Cornell, presumably derived from the medieval Latin phrase for birds of prey, *avis prede*. The scientific name for the bird is *Pandion haliaetus*, and it is of the order Accipitriformes, which includes most of the diurnal birds of prey. Pandion was a mythical Greek king of Athens. While man can be traced back about 1.8 million years, Accipitriformes date back 44 million years.

With a rap sheet like that, one would expect grace, majesty, and beauty. And one would not be disappointed. There is nobility in the way ospreys patiently wait, perched on a pole, and in the way they soar effortlessly through the skies. Observers note that on average it takes about twelve minutes for an osprey to catch a fish—a shorter time than it takes most fishermen.

Paul Spitzer, a conservation biologist who grew up in Old Lyme, was a neighbor and friend of Roger Tory Peterson, who made his home here for almost fifty years. After graduating from Wesleyan, Paul received his PhD from Cornell the year of the first Earth Day in 1970. Conservation became both his avocation and his vocation. For forty-five years he has observed and studied ospreys. While he spends most of the year on the Eastern Shore, he often returns to Old Lyme in summers.

It is Paul Spitzer to whom I owe thanks for the nest erected in the marsh in front of our house—a nest that was occupied within less than a day of its being erected. As he once said, "I think of us on a voyage of understanding." On the first of June, he wrote us of the nests he had been watching, and of the osprey and their love affair with the Connecticut River estuary: "I find spiritual freedom out here in the tideland. I have entered a separate world: sky so blue and crisscrossed with osprey. A succession of males arrive with freshly caught menhaden hanging below in their talons: held parallel to the osprey's flight, thus streamlined. The lowering evening sun illuminates yellow forked menhaden tails, and blood streaming bright from talon wounds. Arriving males hover, scream, and display—which reports the direction and species of fresh prey to others." His words evoke the beauty and the purpose of this estuary.

It is that completeness—the interdependency of nature with its necessary cruelties, the success of evolution, man's role in correcting past faults and so now playing a positive role—that can be observed by those of us lucky to be living in this place. Dr. Spitzer told me that man-made nests were put up not only so that we could be witness to this wonder of nature, but also so that the osprey will know man as a nonthreatening cohabitant.

THE WORLD AT LARGE

I HAVE LONG BEEN INTERESTED IN POLITICS and, in fact, write a twice-weekly "Thought of the Day." I believe that most people want the same things: equal and fair opportunity; justice and the rule of law; the ability to rise in one's chosen vocation or avocation. Where we differ is usually in the means of attaining a common goal. This book—and this section in particular—is meant to be apolitical. There is in this section an essay titled "Partisan Politics." It is the longest essay in the book. While I conclude that differences of opinion are natural, the lack of civility is what makes life in politics so unseemly. If my biases show through, I apologize.

The baker's dozen essays that constitute this section range from the personal—a trip to Texas to see my brother Stuart, and a return to Vienna where my wife and I celebrated our first wedding anniversary—to thoughts about our history, both recent and distant. The attack on 9/11 is the subject of two essays, the first only two days after the event and the second on its tenth anniversary. There are two discussing Memorial Day, but from slightly different perspectives six years apart. There is an essay on my years on Wall Street—a different universe from the place and time where I grew up.

The world is a vast place, yet its effects affect each of us differently.

Thoughts on the Tragedies of September 11
September 13, 2001

I can't go on, I'll go on.

The Unnamable, 1953
Samuel Beckett (1906–1989)

To compare Tuesday's vicious attack on the United States with any other event is to trivialize that act. Has there been another time in American history when our enemies used our civilians to kill our citizens? It will take days, and most likely considerably longer, to fully comprehend the enormity of Tuesday's attack. It is very possible that this heinous action will be seen as one of those seminal events that, in fact, alter history.

There are many reasons for our country's unparalleled prosperity. One of the more important has been the assumption that we were not vulnerable to a direct attack. It has been almost two hundred years (when the British burned the White House during the War of 1812) since the continental United States was directly attacked. That sense of invulnerability came to an end at eight forty-five Tuesday morning, and our lives, as a consequence, will be forever changed. There is also no question that risks still exist because, flush with success, surely beyond their expectations, the perpetrators of Tuesday's tragedies may feel they can do as they please. It is to be hoped that retaliation by the United States will be swift and sure.

The unity that now exists in Congress and among the American people must be harnessed to punish those responsible. Much has been made of World War II's "greatest generation," and nothing that has happened this week diminishes their courage and dedication. However, events dictate actions, and there is no reason to believe that today's younger generation will not rise to the call to defend their country's honor and avenge this act of war. From my perspective, I worry more about the media than I do about the patriotism of young Americans. In my opinion, the members of the fourth estate have taken on a mantle of power that exceeds their innate rights—to keep the public informed by accurately reporting news and expressing their opinions—through irresponsible acts that in fact endanger the security of our country, and by confusing editorial content with news. Anybody who remembers Vietnam knows that to invite video cameras into a theater of military operations is to doom that operation to failure. Anybody who is involved in the stock market and who watches CNBC knows the influence that network has on the markets. The media's influence exceeds their sense of responsibility.

From an economic perspective, this tragedy could not have occurred at a worse time. The economy was already likely in recession. The fact that the four hijacked planes carried a total of 233 passengers (when their capacity must have been closer to one thousand) is indicative of the slowdown. As a consequence of this act of war, travel will almost certainly be curtailed, as will retail sales as people reassess priorities. Capital that might otherwise be deployed will have to be spent replacing the estimated twenty million square feet of lost office space in New York. As for the stock market, we know that we have been in a bear market for the past year and a half in terms of the major indices, and even longer for many stocks. Given the declines we have seen in prices over the last eighteen months, it seems more likely that the real question for the market recovery has more to do with time than with price. In fact, if one assumes that it will take ten years for the NASDAQ Composite to recover to its previous high, that suggests an annualized rate of return of around 11 percent from the current level—close to the long-term average. History suggests that following disasters, the market tends to immediately fall off and then rally back.

However, as indicated at the start of this note, this act of violence was without precedent. Thus history will not be a reliable forecaster. But no one should ever underestimate the resiliency of the American people or their economy and their markets. There is a poem by Robert

Frost in which he says that much as we must mourn the dead, it is the living who must go on living. People will rally. The federal government's stimulative monetary and fiscal policies will continue. The country's economy and markets will revive and thrive.

9/11 Remembered

September 7, 2011

This is not a battle between the United States of America and terrorism, but between the free and democratic world and terrorism.

Tony Blair (1953–)

S UNDAY WILL MARK THE TENTH ANNIVERSARY of 9/11. While it is a day to mourn the dead, and to remember the evil of those who perpetrated this deed, it is also a day to recall the extraordinary heroism of those who fought back on United Flight 93 and those police and firemen who climbed the stairs of the World Trade Center and clambered over the rubble of the Pentagon, sacrificing their lives so that a few could be saved.

The act was deliberate and premeditated. Almost three thousand people died that day, in the Twin Towers, the Pentagon, and a field in Shanksville, Pennsylvania. Unlike the bombing of Pearl Harbor on December 7, 1941, for which closure came long before its tenth anniversary, aboard the USS *Missouri* in Tokyo Bay on September 2, 1945, the terrorist act of ten years ago has had no satisfactory resolution. It is a reason we continue to respect this day, honoring the dead and the heroes, remembering the circumstances, and pursuing revenge. It is true that Osama bin Laden has been killed, as have other leaders of al-Qaeda, but there has been no surrender—no equivalent of VE Day or VJ Day. A war against an amorphous enemy, as George Bush said in its aftermath, is hard to fight and will take decades to complete. Success means preventing further attacks, but the very silence that comes with success makes it difficult to maintain one's guard. But that does not mean that Islamic terrorists are any less evil than conventional enemies of the past, or that they have reformed their ways. It is a war that will require vigilance for decades. There will be no surrender ceremony.

What happened when civilian planes, loaded with innocent people, were turned into weapons cannot be whitewashed. It cannot be forgotten. It cannot be forgiven. While the families of those killed suffered most grievously, the rest of us cannot forget that the killings were an attack on the principles that underlie our democracy—liberty, equality, freedom. Political correctness has put blame on those who water-boarded prisoners, or who acted wrongly at Abu Ghraib prison, but if one really wants to understand torture, read *Unbroken*, Laura Hillenbrand's story of Louis Zamperini's odyssey through a series of Japanese prisoner-of-war camps during World War II. What a few American soldiers did in Iraq was wrong, but none of what they did remotely comes close to real torture, as we have learned through numerous examples, from World War II to Daniel Pearl's beheading in Pakistan in 2002.

We live in a multicultural world, in a country more representative of pan-globalization than any other. We are often described as parochial, isolated from the sophistication of Western Europe, too distant from the poverty of Africa, and insensitive to those of different religions in the Middle East. We are accused of racism and intolerance toward foreign cultures. All of that may be true. But the fact is, as a nation, we are a living manifestation that differences in race and religion can be overcome. Does anyone really believe that the Chinese are more tolerant of outsiders, or that Germans or Brits are more culturally diverse than Americans? No one can (or will) claim that we have arrived at perfect harmony, but no one can deny that we are the world's best example of a "melting pot."

The attack ten years ago promulgated the toppling of the Taliban in Afghanistan, the regime that had harbored al-Qaeda. From this distance in time, it is hard to recall that fear of a repeat of 9/11 was foremost in everyone's minds in the months following the attack. The proliferation of nuclear weapons in those "axis of evil" countries heightened the risk of terrorism. Despite all of today's Monday morning quarterbacking, responsible people in all countries believed that Saddam Hussein was working on a nuclear weapons program. It was known that he had used mustard gas against Iranian soldiers in the Iran-Iraq War of the 1980s and nerve gas to kill thousands of people in the largely Kurdish city of Halabja in Iraq in 1988. The fact that no such weapons were found after the toppling of Saddam created dissension in a nation that had been unified, costing America the moral high ground, at least in the eyes of much of the liberal media and among Mr. Bush's political opponents. The three tiers of the Bush foreign policy—preemption, unilateralism, and hegemony—were replaced with an emphasis on multinationalism that included the odd concept of "leading from behind," a concept that is being tested in Libya today, and throughout the Arab Spring. It will be tested as our troops depart Iraq and Afghanistan; we all hope it works.

Nevertheless, the Obama administration has largely persisted with the Bush policies that have, at least so far, kept our shores free from another attack. The Patriot Act was renewed this past May. The prison at Guantanamo is still in use. An attempt to try terrorists in civilian courts in New York proved unsuccessful. With 7,176 military deaths (4,474 in Iraq and 2,702 in Afghanistan) over the past ten years and with an estimated cost of $2 trillion, the United States is paying a price for its freedom. But liberty is never cheap.

Sunday's services have been marked by controversy. In a decision that can best be described as divisive and insensitive, Mayor Bloomberg has determined that religion should not play a role. That decision stands in sharp contrast to the multisectarian service held at Yankee Stadium shortly after the attack, when Protestant ministers, Catholic priests, Jewish rabbis, Muslim imams, Hindu Brahmans, and Buddhist monks and nuns offered prayers in a remarkable pluralistic tribute to the dead and the living.

Regardless of what politicians do or say on Sunday, it is a day to reflect on our great good luck to live in this country with its foundation of liberty. We owe a great deal to those who have died that we may live in peace. We should never forget the events of that day and how it shocked us from an unhealthy lethargy that had cloaked our insular lives. Oceans separate us from most of the world, but we are neither immune nor impervious. We live in a world filled with risk, but we cannot and do not let it dominate our lives. Unfortunately, there is no perfect protection. Inherent to freedom is an element of discomfiture. Oliver Hardy of Laurel and Hardy fame reportedly said: "Life is not confused, if you know how. But it is muddled."

New Yorker Meets Texan

November 18, 2010

A journey is like a marriage.
The certain way to be wrong is to think you control it.

Travels with Charley, 1962
John Steinbeck (1902–1968)

EVERYONE HAS HAD UNUSUAL TRAVEL experiences. I almost wrote "trips from hell", but that would not be true about mine yesterday. This was just different.

On Tuesday I went to visit my brother Stuart, who three years ago relocated to the flat, but generally ice-free, plains of West Texas in Abilene. He had moved from the decidedly rocky—and often icy—hills of New Hampshire. Stuart suffers from a condition known as Prader-Willi syndrome, which stunts growth, causes obesity, and impacts motor skills. Nevertheless, he is accomplished as an artist. He has exhibited in Boston, New York, and New Hampshire; however, ice, snow, and Stuart do not mix well.

The trip out was uneventful. Not so the return.

My 10:40 a.m. American Eagle flight from Abilene to Dallas was canceled, thereby imperiling my 1:00 p.m. connection to New York. Mechanical trouble was cited as the cause; so my erstwhile plane limped from the gate to wherever they take ailing jets in Abilene. The next two flights were booked solid, but I was promised a seat on the 5:00 p.m. If you have ever been to Abilene, you will know that the idea of spending six hours at its airport, as pleasant as the employees are, is not something you would wish upon your mother-in-law.

So I did the "New Yorky" thing. I booked myself on the 3:30 p.m. from Dallas and called a car service.

That took a while, because car services in Abilene are rare. Nevertheless, the Classic Cab Company came through, but by the time they did I had to cancel the 3:30 p.m. and rebook on the 4:25 p.m., this time upgrading myself to first class, as compensation for the pain and suffering I had already endured.

My driver, Bud Gonzales, who is the owner, showed up about noon—in a white pickup truck for the two-hundred-mile ride to Dallas–Fort Worth Airport. Of course, finding an abandoned, desperate East Coast stranger, he had no compunction about charging New York prices. Given my state, I hardly noticed. Throwing my bag in the bed of the pickup, Bud proceeded to talk his way to Dallas. I learned more than I needed to about his early life in Del Rio and Sanderson and that the common term for one thousand acres is a "section," as in "how many sections does your daddy's ranch encompass?" We passed dozens of ranches, a couple of hills scattered here and there, and the carcasses of several mule deer that had made the mistake of venturing onto I-20.

Other than the lack of a gun rack behind my back, the truck was indistinguishable from most of the other vehicles on the road. I felt like a stranger in my country, much as Dorothy did when she said, "Toto, I've a feeling we're not in Kansas anymore."

Forgetting the size of the DFW airport and not having asked my travel agent for a gate number, I was deposited at terminal C instead of D. However, the satisfaction of rolling up to the first class entrance in a white pickup made the fact that I was at the wrong terminal tolerable. Besides, the sky-train gave me an engineer's view of the airport.

Naturally, the 4:25 p.m. did not take off until 6:35 p.m.—an hour and a half after I should have landed in New York.

Hurricane Irene:
First, Anticipation, and Then, Her Power
August 29, 2011

The wind shows how close to the edge we are.

Slouching Towards Bethlehem, 2008
Joan Didion (1934–)

FRIDAY WAS EERIE IN RUMSON, NEW JERSEY. The day was warm—perhaps a little too humid—with a clear blue sky. But the knowledge that a major storm was approaching cast a foreboding tone. The waves were a little rougher than usual—the normal green flag at the beach had been replaced by yellow—but still okay for my grandchildren, who kept dashing into the waves and then letting the tide carry them back onto the sand.

Nevertheless, with Irene approaching, the decision was made that afternoon to close the club for the weekend, an obvious decision as Governor Chris Christie had mandated an evacuation of the entire New Jersey coast.

There is a sense of helplessness one feels when confronted with a storm like Irene. Bicycles and toys are stored. Porch, terrace, and pool furniture is moved under cover; shutters are tightened, plate glass taped, and cars tucked in garages. But one's house remains exposed, as do the trees that have stood for decades providing shade in the summer and protection from nosy neighbors year-round. One cannot be assured that shingles will not be torn from the roof by wet, wind-blown gusts approaching at a hundred miles an hour. Friday was, as the saying goes, the calm before the storm.

For the past thirty-odd years, we have rented a house during the month of August in the town of Rumson, New Jersey, where my wife, Caroline, spent her summers growing up. The house we were in is a wonderful old place built around the turn of the previous century, located about a half mile from the beach. There was no concern about the ocean breaching the area, as the land is high and Rumson is separated from the ocean by the Shrewsbury River. There was, however, a concern—a concern that was realized—about losing power.

So late Friday we made some decisions. My son and his family would return to Connecticut; Caroline would stay with a childhood friend who possessed a generator; I would return to New York.

But it was the eeriness of the calm on Friday, mimicked in the stillness of the air, that riveted my attention. Such reactions are not uncommon when impending storms approach—even those that are man-made. French nobles in the late 1780s had to know they were unpopular with the public, as did aristocrats in tsarist Russia in the months leading up to the revolution of 1917. In the months leading up to the credit crisis in 2007–2008, market volatility dropped and a sense of complacency descended on Wall Street, undetected by all but a few.

However, it is the indiscriminate power that characterizes nature that instills an innate sense of fear. Storms such as Irene cannot be harnessed; we cannot alter their direction; a single storm possesses more energy than man has been able to muster since he exited the cave. They attack rich and poor, black and white, Muslims and Christians—they show no quarter, heed no master, and abide by no rules man has created.

We sat on the beach on Friday, realizing Irene was coming and that Americans would die because of her, yet knowing we were powerless to stop her. Irene is just one more reminder of man's insignificance in nature's larger scheme. One is reminded of the Earl of Gloucester in the first scene of Act IV of *King Lear*:

> *I' th' last night's storm I such a fellow saw,*
> *Which made me think a man a worm. My son*
> *Came then into my mind, and yet my mind*
> *Was then scarce friends with him. I have heard more since.*
> *As flies to wanton boys are we to th' gods;*
> *They kill us for their sport.*

As I sat alone in my apartment in New York surfing channels on Saturday afternoon, it was readily apparent that Mayor Bloomberg's failure to prepare for the big blizzard last December would not be repeated as Irene roared north. The lesson had been learned. It is better to be over- than underprepared. Mayors and governors outdid one another in ordering mandatory evacuations. People in low-lying areas were inconvenienced, but caution proved successful in that human tragedies, throughout the path of the storm, were limited. Any death is to be regretted, and certainly the twenty or so whose deaths were attributed to Irene are mourned. But when one considers that the sweep of this storm, with its 500-mile wingspan, affected sixty-five million people, the loss of life was minimal.

(My personal high point on Saturday was seeing on ABC News four of my grandchildren sitting in their minivan at a rest stop on the Garden State Parkway, as their mother, my daughter-in-law, was interviewed about their return to Connecticut from the New Jersey shore.)

Man has the ability to forecast and track hurricanes, but we cannot divert them. But anticipation saves lives, as happened in this instance. In contrast, there was little preparation for the infamous New England Hurricane of '38, which hit Long Island with winds of 115 miles per hour and then swept across New England, seventy-three years ago. That storm, admittedly larger, caused 682 deaths.

As Irene passed overhead on Sunday, the sun reappeared briefly, prior to sinking into the west. That reappearance was like an apology for the inconvenience she had caused, but the message remained clear: no matter what technology we create, no matter what pollution we generate or what weapons we develop, nature is bigger than any of us, individually or collectively. It is a sobering thought.

A Return to Vienna

June 30, 2008

If you start to take Vienna—take Vienna.

Napoleon Bonaparte (1769–1821)

Love: a temporary insanity curable by marriage.

The Devil's Dictionary, 1911
Ambrose Bierce (1842–1914)

FORTY-THREE YEARS AND SIXTY-EIGHT days after celebrating our first wedding anniversary at Restaurant Griechenbeisl in Vienna, Caroline and I returned on June 18. We were accompanied by a good friend and his parents, both of whom were Vienna-born. I brought visa photos that had been taken forty-three years earlier. My friend indicated that the restaurant, Vienna's oldest, had not changed; Caroline, he pointed out, looks identical today to her photo of forty-three years earlier, but I am unrecognizable from my photo. However, whatever alteration the body may have undergone, in mind and spirit I feel the same. While cognizant of the past, and casting an eye toward the future, I live in the present.

Vienna seems to be of like mind. It has reverence for its past as the classical music capital of the world—a city where Mozart, Beethoven, Johann Strauss (both senior and junior), Joseph Haydn, and Johannes Brahms lived, wrote, and practiced their music. It was the capital of the Austro-Hungarian Empire (1867–1918), an aggregation that emerged from the Austrian Empire (1804–1867), which in turn had been founded by Holy Roman Emperor Francis II (who became Emperor Francis I of Austria). A hundred years ago it sat at the center of an empire consisting of sixty million people—an empire that had been achieved largely through marriage, not war. The Hapsburg women were supposedly so prolific that, as we were told by a guide, they were referred to as baby machines. Daughters married heirs to thrones in places such as Spain, Naples, Romania, and Czechoslovakia; many of these rulers then chose to cast their lot with the Hapsburgs.

World War I—in many respects the most tragic of all European wars—was ignited by the assassination on June 28, 1914, of Archduke Franz Ferdinand, nephew of Emperor Franz Joseph and heir to the Hapsburg throne. Four and a half years and twenty million deaths later, Europe was devastated. Austria had lost an emperor and an empire. Vienna, which had been capital to sixty million citizens, was now capital to about six million Austrians.

The years between the wars (the First Republic) were dominated initially by Karl Renner and the Social Democrats, then increasingly by right-wing parties. Hopes for peace and democracy evaporated as economic depression enveloped the globe. By 1934 Austrian Fascists essentially imposed a dictatorship; on March 12, 1938, the Germans annexed Austria in a bloodless Anschluss. Fascism and Nazism emerged in Europe to fill a leadership vacuum, taking advantage of, and adding to, rising nationalism and economic fear that had become ubiquitous throughout much of the world. My friends' parents were fortunate to emigrate (though "fortunate" seems too a gentle euphemism, as they had to leave behind everything they could not carry). Hitler's armies occupied this proud city, which had produced, besides the musicians named above, the Spanish Riding School with its magnificent Lipizzaner stallions, Sigmund Freud, St. Stephen's Cathedral, and the Sacher torte—a city that had governed an empire whose antecedents preceded the unification of Germany in 1871 by a thousand years. By war's end many of the city's structures were in rubble and its Jewish population of two hundred thousand had shrunk to five thousand.

During the long years of the Cold War, Vienna served as a salient in the line demarking the East from the West. Similar to Berlin, Vienna was divided, though less imperiled. It served as home to transients making their way from the suffocation of Communism to opportunities in the West, a situation depicted in the 1949 British film noir

The Third Man, starring Joseph Cotten and Orson Welles. Ten years after the war, the Soviets suddenly and without explanation departed, and Austria's renaissance began. The Austrian State Treaty, relieving Austria of foreign occupation, was signed on May 15, 1955, at Belvedere Palace. Dr. Leopold Figl, Austria's foreign minister (and former chancellor), stepped to the balcony and proclaimed to the crowd below, "*Osterreich ist frei!* [Austria is free!]"

Much of Europe's economic growth is dependent upon former Eastern Bloc countries, with their natural resources and an ambitious population eager to raise its standard of living. Vienna's geographic position proved to be of strategic importance as the city bridged the gap between old Europe and new. Today that location puts it near the center of the European Union. As of this writing the EU comprises twenty-seven member states[1] and 500 million people, and as the union gradually expands south and east, Vienna's strategic center will become even more obvious.

The city is lively, catering to tourists and business alike. It is a dynamic and optimistic place whose people enjoy life amidst its coffee shops and opera houses. And, of course, over the past couple of weeks it has been serving as host for Euro 2008, the Continent's quadrennial soccer championship.

The Soviets had been gone for ten years by the time Caroline and I arrived in April 1965. However, dinginess within the city betrayed the earlier Soviet occupation. Its beauty lay beneath a grimy surface. Today that grime is all gone. A significant portion of the inner ring has been set aside for pedestrians. High-end Western retailers abide within historic buildings and alongside local stores of ancient lineage. In a city noted for its coffeehouses, Starbucks has found a place. Commercialization has been done tastefully, and its four opera houses continue to produce some of the world's best music. The Lipizzaner stallions in the Spanish Riding School live as magnificently as ever.

---

1. Croatia joined in 2013, bringing the number of member states to twenty-eight.

Above all, Vienna is a city for lovers, and so provided a perfect venue for Caroline and myself rejoicing in forty-four years of marriage. And, oh! There were times when even Ambrose Bierce got it wrong.

Memorial Day in Old Lyme

May 30, 2007

In Flanders fields the poppies blow
Between the crosses, row on row,
That mark our place; and in the sky
The larks, still bravely singing, fly
Scarce heard amid the guns below.

"In Flanders Fields," 1915
John McRae (1872–1918)

We cherish, too, the poppy red
That grows on fields where valor led;
It seems to signal to the skies
That blood of heroes never dies.

"We Shall Keep the Faith," 1918
Written in response to "In Flanders Fields"
Moina Michael (1869–1944)[2]

T HE MONTH OF MAY has always been a favorite time. It is a fitting season to celebrate one of our great holidays—Memorial Day. The promise of spring, which first hints at its impending arrival on warm winter days, climaxes during the month. May begins with vestiges of winter still visible in leafless trees and a flowerless garden. By Memorial Day our maples gently shimmer in their new greens under a beaming sun.

---

2. Poppies are traditionally worn by the British on Remembrance Day (November 11) to honor those who died during World War I; however, Moina Michael was an American who was born and lived in Georgia, and the sentiments she expressed are universal in their appeal.

As I sit in the garden on the Sunday before the holiday with roses in full bloom and peonies about to explode, birds singing, church bells ringing, and the sound of the train to Boston whistling in the distance, it feels right to pause for a moment in remembrance of those who have fallen so we may live. What once hibernated has reawakened. Scientists may be able to explain in excruciating detail the manner in which plants seemingly die in the fall and are reborn in the spring, but to most of us their reappearance is a miracle. Two days ago, in an unintended act of preparation for Memorial Day, I spent the morning killing weeds in the driveway. Yesterday, in an act of contrition, I spent an hour watering our roses.

Memorial Day has its origins in the years that followed the Civil War. In 1868, General John Logan, commander-in-chief of the Grand Army of the Republic, declared May 30 of that year as Decoration Day—a day of remembrance. Following World War I, the holiday became Memorial Day, a day to honor all fallen American soldiers. In 1971, the last Monday in May was designated as the annual observance of Memorial Day.

This year overcast skies greeted the dawn—perfect for a day of somber reflection. In a small town, the highlight of Memorial Day is the parade. Old Lyme is a village of 7,500 people (9,500 if one includes Lyme). It doubles during the summer. On Lyme Street, the route of the parade, one sees neighbors and friends among the audience and the marchers. Ice cream cones and Bloody Marys abound (among the audience, not the marchers—and usually not in the hands of the same person).

In our town the parade begins at 11:00 a.m., assembling near the Old Lyme Art Academy before marching up Main Street past the barbershop, town hall, library, and Congregational church. This year, as always, veterans led the way. It is a small group. It includes a few older

men who served during World War II, a couple of younger people who have recently returned from Iraq, and others who served in Korea and Vietnam. They are followed by the high school marching band, Boy Scouts, Girl Scouts, Little League teams, a five-man fife-and-drum group from Deep River, Scottish bagpipes from Mystic, Cub Scouts, Brownies, fire engines, ambulances, antique cars, and numerous pre-teens on their bicycles. The parade ends at the Duck River Cemetery. Within its confines lie the remains of men who served in every war in which America fought, from King Philip's War to Vietnam.

As the melancholy echo of taps reverberates through the trees, across the marshes and over the tombstones, we are reminded of the debt the rest of us owe to those who served and died. The expressions on the faces of marchers and onlookers alike are reminders that those who did die did not do so in vain.

Memorial Day 2013
May 27, 2013

*I thought about a graveyard
At the bottom of the sea,
Of unmarked graves in Arlington.
No, freedom is not free.*

"Freedom Is Not Free," 1981
Kelly Strong

FREEDOM IS NOT FREE. Freedom is the goal. War is its means. And war extracts a terrible and treasured price. In his famous address delivered on Memorial Day 1895 at Harvard University, Oliver Wendell Holmes Jr. spoke of the faith of soldiers—in themselves, their leaders, and their country. A year earlier he had talked of how in his youth "our hearts were touched with fire." In 1895, thirty years after the end of the Civil War, he had no illusions about an eternal peace on earth. His observations ring with relevance today: "War, when you are at it, is horrible and dull. . . . I hope it may be long before we are called again to sit at that master's feet. But some teacher of the kind we all need. In this snug, over-safe corner of the world we need it, that we may realize that our comfortable routine is no eternal necessity of things, but merely a little space of calm in the midst of the tempestuous streaming of the world. . . . Out of heroism grows faith in the worth of heroism." It is a message that indeed has relevance for today.

After graduation from Harvard, the young Holmes had served in the Massachusetts Twentieth from 1861 to 1864. He was wounded three times: at Ball's Bluff, Antietam, and Chancellorsville, concluding his service with the rank of captain.

Originally called Decoration Day, for the flowers that were laid on newly dug graves in 1864, the observance soon became a national holiday. May 30 was selected, as it was deemed the optimal date for flowers to be in bloom. By the 1880s it had begun to be called Memorial Day. When I was growing up in the late 1940s and early 1950s, Memorial Day was a celebration of American exceptionalism whose purpose was to uphold freedom throughout the world. The soldiers who marched then, to the accompaniment of a fife-and-drum corps and high school bands, were young veterans from the Second World War and grizzled veterans of the First. As I accompanied them on my bicycle to the Grove Street Cemetery in Peterborough, a surge of pride brought a lump to my throat. It still does, as much smaller cadres of soldiers march and ride in Old Lyme's Memorial Day Parade. They were and are reminders of the incalculable debt we owe to those who gave so much in order that we can live freely and securely.

In 1971 the date was moved to the fourth Monday in May, allowing for a three-day weekend. We do gain something when holidays are thus moved, but we lose the intensity of and some of the reason for the celebration.

Over the past few years it has become habitual (perhaps becoming traditional) for my oldest son and his family to join Caroline and me in Old Lyme for Memorial Day weekend. Children and grandchildren are reminders of the continuum of life—that while we live in the present, we must be reminded of those who came before and those who will follow. Memorial Day is a fitting holiday for families. Television and the Internet have changed the relationships between soldiers and civilians. Vietnam was the first war brought into our living rooms, and the country's attitude toward war was forever changed. My grandchildren are too young to recognize both the horror and honor that war bestows. But observing them watching real soldiers make their way up Lyme Street to the Duck River Cemetery, I pray that the same chills I felt more than sixty years ago will tingle their spines—that they will recognize that sacrifice is a gift from people just like them.

In his 1895 Memorial Day speech at Harvard, Justice Holmes concluded his remarks with the thought that part of the soldier's faith is, having known great things, to be content with silence. He then quoted lines sung by a "warlike people" along the Danube:

> *"For the spring has come and the earth has smiled,*
> *And the dead must be forgot."*
> *Then the soldier spake from the deep dark grave:*
> *"I am content."*

It is well that soldiers be content with silence, but it is not proper that we, the beneficiaries of their sacrifice, should be so as well. No matter which day we celebrate the gift of freedom they gave us, and no matter what we call it, remembrance of the fallen is something we should all honor.

The Fourth of July

July 3, 2013

I'm proud to be an American
Where at least I know I'm free.
And I won't forget the men who died,
Who gave that right to me.

"God Bless the USA," 1984
Lee Greenwood (1942–)

In the truest sense, freedom cannot be bestowed; it must be achieved.

Franklin D. Roosevelt (1982–1945)

MOST YEARS, JULY FOURTH ARRIVES HOT and sticky. We celebrate with cookouts, going to the beach, playing softball, and watching fireworks in the evening. Since 1889, when my great-great-grandfather noted in his diary "Children and grandchildren played baseball," my father's family has played softball at his home outside of Boston. It is pleasant and comfortable being with friends and family. But it is light-years away from a similarly muggy day in Philadelphia when representatives of the thirteen states met 237 years ago.

We are a fortunate people who live in freedom, with little sense of how many have died to retain it and less knowledge of how difficult it was to forge. It is easy to take liberty for granted when we never had to fight for it. While we watch from afar street demonstrations in Cairo, Israel's constant struggle for survival, and a civil war in Syria, we should remember why we celebrate this day. The United States had its own civil war, fought to hold together a nation rent by the abomination that was slavery, a denial of the very essence that all men are created equal.

Today marks the sesquicentennial of the major turning point in the Civil War—Gettysburg. Of the approximately 164,000 soldiers from both sides who took part, almost 8,000 were killed or died of their wounds in the three days of battle. Another 27,000 were wounded, and 11,000 were captured or missing. In Monday's *Wall Street Journal*, Allen Guelzo, professor at Gettysburg College, noted that Lincoln heard of the victory on July 4, which he saw as a "symbolic coincidence." It was, Professor Guelzo says of Lincoln, as though a bright line had been drawn between the moment in 1776 when a new nation's representatives first declared as a "self-evident truth that all men are created equal" and 1863 when "the cohorts of those who opposed that declaration that all men are created equal had turned tail and run."

More than anything, July 4 represents the birth of a nation. In the summer of 1776, fifty-six representatives of about 2.5 million people from the thirteen colonies met in Philadelphia, which, at about 40,000, was the country's largest city. The Second Continental Congress on July 2 approved the newly written Declaration of Independence. Early on the morning of the fourth, church bells rang throughout Philadelphia, signaling that the Declaration of Independence had been adopted. The Boston Tea Party, Paul Revere's ride, Lexington and Concord, and the Battle of Bunker Hill were all in the past. The crossing of the Delaware and the battles fought at Monmouth, Brandywine, Charlestown, and Yorktown were all in the future. It would be seven years before the British finally gave up and sailed for home.

A few weeks after the Declaration, 427 British warships carrying 1,200 cannon, 34,000 British and Hessian troops, and 10,000 sailors appeared off Long Island and in New York Harbor. Facing the greatest army and navy in the world were Generals George Washington and Nathanael Greene, with about 5,000 ill-trained volunteer troops. The Revolution was about to begin in earnest.

The process toward independence had taken many years. It was not easy for most colonists. Familial and business ties linked Americans to England. The French and Indian War had concluded barely a dozen years earlier with Britain dominating the eastern half of North America. About half the residents of the American colonies in 1776 were British by heritage. (Interestingly, but not surprisingly, the second-largest

group was Africans.) Virtually all the signers of the Declaration of Independence were British. Being a member of the Commonwealth was seen by many as a positive thing. The British navy protected ships engaged in commerce and trade. The relationship was symbiotic. Englishmen and -women served as customers for goods produced in America and in turn supplied finer clothing, clocks, and china.

Rebellion was a serious step. Had the Revolution failed, there is little question that all of the leaders would have been hanged as traitors—their lives and their fortunes would have been forfeited. The decision to rebel was seen by Loyalists as an act of treason. For men of wealth—and most of the signatories to the Declaration were wealthy—joining the Revolution was an all-or-nothing decision. Failure would mean death for themselves and penury for their heirs. It could not have been an easy decision. In his concise, readable, and fact-filled short history *Revolutionary Summer*, Joseph Ellis tracks the events from May to October 1776. Professor Ellis shows how consensus was reached in the weeks before Philadelphia. The debates covered everything from the moral integrity of the Revolution, to slavery and the status of women, to broadening the electorate to include men without property. Benjamin Franklin cautioned against independence until after a new government had been formed. While the New England colonies were early to declare independence, it was only late in the process that Pennsylvania and New York endorsed the concept, with New York's delegation voting in favor a week after the Continental Congress approved the Declaration.

John Dickinson of Pennsylvania was a reluctant revolutionary, as were many, especially in the mid-Atlantic states. Gillian Tett, in last weekend's *Financial Times*, wrote of a recent book, *The Founding Conservatives: How a Group of Unsung Heroes Saved the American Revolution* by David Lefer. These were men who were part of the elite, but who were determined to protect their privilege. They were not loyal to the crown, but they did not want to see the country fall into anarchy. Their enlistment was critical, and much credit goes to John Dickinson, who anonymously published *Letters from a Farmer in Pennsylvania*.

In them, he defended the concepts of liberty and freedom, but in the context of property rights, the rule of law, and free-market capitalism. Mr. Dickinson, according to Ms. Tett, was considered the most trusted man in America. In 1768 he penned the following lines, which became even more resonant once he committed to the Revolution:

Then join hand in hand, brave Americans all!
By uniting we stand, by dividing we fall.

The more one reads about the era—and tosses myths and stories overboard—the more it becomes apparent that it is not just a miracle we celebrate, but the extraordinary efforts by a small group of people who were able to convince the majority of the righteousness of their belief. As well, we must acknowledge that the leaders—Washington, Adams, Jefferson, Franklin, Dickinson, Madison, and many others—knew full well that should they fail they would be hanged as traitors. As it was, there were about 50,000 casualties during the war, of whom about 8,000 died in combat. That may not sound like a lot over eight years, but keep in mind that the population of the colonies was 2.5 million. A comparable number of dead and wounded today would be 6.5 million.

But the consequence of their bravery and determination is that we live in the freest nation the world has ever known. Ronald Reagan spoke often of a "city on a hill." It was an image recycled from a 1630 sermon by John Winthrop (later governor of the Massachusetts Bay Colony). Winthrop, in turn, borrowed the words from the Bible and Jesus' Sermon on the Mount. In his farewell address in 1989, President Reagan described what he meant by those words: "It was a tall, proud city built on rocks stronger than oceans . . . a city with free ports that hummed with commerce and creativity. And if there had to be city walls, the walls had doors and the doors were open to anyone with the will and the heart to get here." It is an image to be remembered as immigration is debated in Congress.

Democracy can be fragile, ephemeral, and inefficient. Democracy only works when people take an interest. It cannot be taken for granted. Complacency infects even the hardiest. An exacerbated Thomas Jefferson once declaimed: "My God! How little do my countrymen know what blessings they are in possession of, and which no other people enjoy."

Freedom is not free. It is demanding. "What we obtain too cheap," observed Thomas Paine in December 1776, "we esteem too lightly." But it is, as Moshe Dayan once said, "the oxygen of the soul." In 1779, Paine wrote: "Those who expect the blessings of freedom, must, like men, undergo the fatigue of supporting it." As we enjoy our liberty, we must also be ever vigilant, especially regarding a government that trends toward dependency and erodes personal responsibility. In *Man and Superman*, George Bernard Shaw wrote, "Liberty means responsibility—that is why most men dread it."

Nevertheless, the strength of the country has always been in its people and the knowledge that they will, when pushed hard enough, fight back and do the right thing. That has been the case for 237 years. The long-term survival of our country depends on the Spirit of '76 being alive in '13. So whether you spend the day at the beach, barbecuing with your family, or participating in a Coney Island hot-dog-eating contest; whether you are pitching a softball to the granddaughter of your second cousin or sitting on the bank of the Hudson River watching New York City's fireworks, remember the reason you are able to do so. Think of those who died at Valley Forge, at the Alamo, at Antietam, on San Juan Hill, at Belleau Wood, on Riva Ridge, at Chosin Reservoir, and the Battle of Hue. Remember those who continue to fight for our freedom—those who have fought and died in Iraq and Afghanistan, and those who have been grievously wounded. It is because of them that we are at liberty to enjoy the freedom to picnic with our friends and family. None of those who died would want us to spend the day in mourning, but respect requires that we think of them and that we honor the principle of freedom for which they fought, and be unafraid of the responsibility that comes from self-reliance.

Happy Fourth!

Veterans Day 2009
November 11, 2009

Honor to the soldier and sailor everywhere, who bravely bears his country's cause. Honor, also, to the citizen who cares for his brother in the field and serves, as best he can, the same cause.

Abraham Lincoln (1809–1865)

O N THE ELEVENTH HOUR (GMT) of this date ninety-one years ago, the firing ceased and the "war to end all wars" came to an end, but not before an estimated sixteen million were killed and twenty-one million wounded over four years and three months of utter horror.

The day is celebrated in much of the world as Remembrance Day, a fitting title as the war destroyed a generation of British, French, German, and Russian youth. An English gentleman I know, a graduate of Oxford, once told me of photographs of his college's team captains hung on a wall there. Of the young men depicted in more than twenty photographs for the class of 1914, only one survived.

The war marked the end of tsarist Russia, the Austro-Hungarian Empire, and the German Kaiser. The map of Europe changed, with Russia renouncing claims to Poland and the Baltic countries—Latvia, Lithuania, and Estonia. The new countries of Yugoslavia and Czechoslovakia were carved from the Austrian and German empires respectively. Austria and Hungary were established as independent countries.

The war also produced some of the most beautiful poetry ever written, by young men like Wilfred Owen, Rupert Brooke, John McCrae, Isaac Rosenberg, and Edward Thomas, none of whom survived the war. Alan Seeger, an American poet and author of those haunting lines "I have a rendezvous with death/At some disputed barricade," was killed in 1917 at Belloy-en-Santerre. Roland Leighton, engaged to Vera Brittain (who later wrote the evocative *Testament of Youth*), was killed on December 23, 1915, at Louvencourt, France. With my wife, my son Sydney, and his wife, Beatriz, I visited his grave in October 2000.

One of the best-known poems is "In Flanders Fields," written in May and published on December 8, 1915, by John McCrae. The middle stanza reads:

> *We are the Dead. Short days ago*
> *We lived, felt dawn, saw sunset glow,*
> *Loved and were loved, and now we lie*
> *In Flanders fields.*

War is the most serious event of one's life and yet can seem so wasteful. On the signing of the armistice, on November 11, 1918, Thomas Hardy wrote a poem: "And There Was a Great Calm." The final stanza reads:

> *Calm fell. From Heaven distilled a clemency;*
> *There was peace on earth and silence in the sky:*
> *Some could, some could not, shake off misery:*
> *The Sinister Spirit sneered: "It had to be!"*
> *And again the Spirit of Pity whispered, "Why?"*

Europe, in the first decade of the twentieth century, was prosperous. Trade was expanding. Electricity, automobiles, the telephone, and other products of the Industrial Revolution were dramatically altering and improving the average family's life. The old monarchies in Germany, Austria, and Russia were visibly failing, as democracy relentlessly marched onward. Yet the guns of August thundered in 1914.

There were no evil men. Propaganda turned the Kaiser into a killer of Belgian babies, but he was no Hitler. It was the absence of war, and then its romanticizing, that drove so many to enlist. Other than the Franco-Prussian conflict, war had been largely absent from the

European continent since Napoleon had been exiled to St. Helena ninety-nine years earlier—so the horrors of war had been erased from memory. It had been a remarkable period of peace on a continent that had been at war for most of the previous thousand years. It was this innocence, coming at a time of remarkable prosperity and general goodwill among nations, that made this war so awful.

There is no such thing as a "good" war. There are wars that are justifiable and there are others that are not. Often, it is only with the distance of time that we can truly tell the difference. Nazism was worth eradicating; yet had it not been for the First World War, there might well never have been the need for a second. That is part of the tragedy of 1914.

The most difficult and lonely decision a president can make is to commit troops to combat, yet there are times when he must. Time will judge his decision. As difficult as it may be for those of us leading comfortable, peaceful lives, and as distant we are from the roar of guns, we have a democratic system worth defending and preserving. Today we have soldiers committed to that end in Iraq and Afghanistan.

Whatever we call today—Veterans Day, Armistice Day, Remembrance Day—we must honor it, remember the fallen and remember the reasons for the conflict. We owe a debt of gratitude to our armed services. We have an allegiance to those who fought, wept, and died in past wars, so that today we may enjoy, laugh, and live.

Forty Years on Wall Street

September 5, 2007

Oh the great days, in the distance enchanted,
Days of fresh air, in the rain and the sun,
How we rejoiced as we struggled and panted—
Hardly believable, forty years on!

*

Forty years on, growing older and older,
Shorter in wind, as in memory long.

Words from the song "Forty Years On," 1872
Edward Ernest Bowen and John Farmer

THIS MONTH MARKS THE COMPLETION of my first forty years on Wall Street. In many respects, it seems but a moment since I entered Training Class #105 at Merrill Lynch's offices on Pine Street in lower Manhattan. On the other hand, the enormity of changes in the capital markets speaks to the years gone by. At the end of the summer of 1967—a summer dubbed by the press the "summer of love"—I left my job with Eastman Kodak to try my hand as a stockbroker. My boss, when I informed him of my plans, told me what a mistake I was making. "In forty years," I remember him saying, "you would be a vice president, living in Rochester and making $40,000 a year." I responded that those were three reasons for changing careers.

Charles Handy, in *The Age of Unreason*, wrote that "change, after all, is only another word for growth." And it is disruptive change that is most creative—creative destruction, as first described by Joseph Schumpeter more than sixty years ago. Certainly the last forty years have seen substantial change: in 1972 the dollar became no longer anchored to gold; on May 1, 1975, negotiated commissions replaced fixed commissions on the New York Stock Exchange; Regulation Q interest-rate restrictions were phased out; oil prices rose substantially, igniting inflation and higher interest rates.

At the same time great strides were made in technology. One result of these seemingly disparate events was the growth of derivatives, particularly the use of futures, which in turn gave birth to index funds. An early benefit for the markets of the increased speed of computers and the reduction in commission rates was volume, which when I started in the business ran less than ten million shares a day. In the summer of 1982, I addressed the training class at Salomon Brothers; I recall asking rhetorically why one would want to go into the equity business with the Dow Jones Industrial Average selling 15 percent below where it had been fifteen years earlier and commissions a fraction of what they had been. The answer (besides the obvious, which was that stocks were cheap) was volume, which had increased sixfold over that period and looked to go higher. Technological advances had allowed the NYSE, which was incapable of handling ten million shares a day in the late 1960s, to easily process ten times that number.

As the markets soared in the mid-1980s, institutional investors with memories of the 1970s fresh in their minds leapt at the possibility of hedging their equity positions through "portfolio insurance." In turn, the idea of an "insured" portfolio gave unwarranted confidence to these same managers, whose faith was shattered on a Monday morning in October 1987. The Federal Reserve played an active role in an attempt to restore confidence, as did senior Wall Street executives. While it took another two years for the indices to exceed their 1987 highs, analysts by November of that year were raising estimates for 1988. In response, the exchange introduced circuit breakers, which get triggered initially by moves up or down greater than 2 percent, with the idea of limiting daily damage, and portfolio insurance became a historical footnote. However, the growth in derivatives continued unimpeded.

Technology and communication are certainly responsible for the major changes I have seen over the past forty years. Volume has increased to undreamt-of levels, and it has become virtually impossible to distance oneself from the pervasive nature of an unrelenting market. There is almost no place one can escape from CNBC and Bloomberg and the ubiquitous BlackBerry and its cousin the cell phone. A defining characteristic of our time, brought forth by developments in technology and communication, is the emphasis on the short term. We see it in day traders, though their numbers have dwindled since the halcyon days of the late 1990s. Television is for surfing. Two-minute YouTube videos have replaced thirty-minute documentaries. Two-minute dating has become standard fare.

Yet despite this cultural emphasis on the short term, important decisions for most people remain of a long-term nature—college and courses of study, friendships, marriage, jobs, investing, where to live, where and how to retire. These decisions require a longer-term perspective, and it is the unchanging human emotions that I believe are most important. People, at the core, don't change that much. Greed, fear, love, hate, anxiety, and envy have been around as long as we have, and they continue to drive investment decisions. Emotions expressed by characters in the plays of Shakespeare, the stories of Dickens, or the poems of Whitman are as real and as relevant today as when they were written.

It has been a great forty years, and I feel fortunate in my life. I have met, known, and worked with some of the legends of the industry. While my children were neither encouraged nor discouraged from entering the business, my two sons have spent the last thirteen years in the financial field—one, Sydney, as owner of his own firm, and the other, Edward, as a securities analyst. My daughter, Linie, who has a master's in education, was the sole holdout until she married a securities analyst, Bill Featherston. So, for better or worse the family is tied to the fortunes of the industry, an industry that continues to change. Schumpeter's theory of creative destruction is being tested once again, this time in the housing and mortgage finance markets. History suggests that today's turmoil will cause a different and better future. Like Stuart Little on his quest, change remains a constant in our lives. It is one of the challenges that make our lives interesting. When asked why I continue to work, I reply that I love it, especially the challenge of the markets and the human interaction. Recognizing that the future belongs to the young, I plan to be around as long as the people I work with will have me.

A Cradle of Civilization
April 17, 2013

While civilization has been improving our houses,
it has not equally improved the men who are to inhabit them.

Henry David Thoreau (1817–1862)

A S ALL SCHOOLCHILDREN KNOW, the Cradle of Civilization usually refers to Mesopotamia, a region centered on the city of Har-
put in eastern Turkey, in that fertile crescent between the Tigris and
Euphrates Rivers. It extends down into the Kurdish region of Iraq.
While it was home to the first written records, it is an area that has
seen much violence over the years. Bostonians, in the years following
the American Revolution, looked upon themselves as the New World's
"Cradle of Civilization."

The designation was not unwarranted. The greater Boston area is
home to the nation's oldest university, Harvard, and to more than a
hundred other universities. The Boston Symphony and Boston Pops
are world-renowned. There are forty-plus museums, perhaps the most
famous of which is the Isabella Stewart Gardner Museum. The concept
of a Cradle of Civilization lay behind the Transcendentalists, a group
that was formed in the 1830s. It included such notables as Henry David
Thoreau, Ralph Waldo Emerson, Walt Whitman, John Muir, Elizabeth
Peabody, William Ellery Channing, Amos Bronson Alcott, and his
more famous daughter, Louisa May. They were idealists who believed
in the inherent goodness of people and nature, but that society and its
institutions (especially political parties) ultimately corrupted the puri-
ty of the individual. Self-reliance and independence were the charac-
teristics they most highly valued. They would have been shocked, but
perhaps not surprised, by the horrific events in Boston on Monday.

The building that came to symbolize Boston's Cradle of Civilization
was Faneuil Hall. It was built in the middle of the eighteenth century

and quickly became a gathering place for those who would become known as patriots, as they protested the growing presence of the British army. When the Revolution erupted in 1775, the first blood was shed at Concord Bridge in Lexington. Patriots' Day commemorates that first battle fought on April 19. This state holiday includes a home game for the Boston Red Sox and the running of the Boston Marathon, and has been celebrated since 1969 on the third Monday in April. The Boston Marathon, America's oldest and most fabled, was first run in 1896.

The fact that terrorists would use that venue to kill and maim innocent men, women, and children makes one reconsider the concept of civilization and a civilized society. The term civilized has long been associated with violence. Indigenous groups, whether they were Visigoths, Celts, Aztecs, or Native Americans, were often killed by "civilizing" conquerors.

What is civilization? When asked about Western civilization, Mahatma Gandhi responded, "I think it would be a very good idea." In *The Philosophy of Civilization*, published in 1923, Albert Schweitzer defines civilization as being "the sum total of all progress made by man in every sphere of action and from every point of view, in so far as that progress helps towards the spiritual perfecting of individuals as the progress of all progress." I don't even know what that means. I prefer to take my medicine in simpler dosages. Webster's first dictionary (1828) defines civilization thus: "The state of being refined in manners from the grossness of savage life, and improved in arts and sciences." From having worked on trading floors for the better part of five decades, I suspect Noah Webster would have noted a reversion to savagery in much of the "civilized" world of late.

The word *civil* derives from the Latin *civilis*, which relates to a citizen or townsman as opposed to a soldier, the concept being that citizens were more courteous than soldiers. *Civil service* referred to jobs performed by civilian employees of governments in foreign countries, as opposed to occupying troops. Nevertheless, a lack of civility has become ubiquitous in the last hundred years, as war extended from the battlefield into living rooms. Gas emitted from trenches on both sides in World War II followed the wind, which sometimes headed toward the enemy, but might drift over a field of cattle, or into a nearby village. When Germany bombed London during the early months of World War II, its purpose was to kill civilians, so as to dishearten the population. More than 28,000 Londoners died over an eight-month period. During three days in February 1945, Allied bombers killed about 25,000 citizens of Dresden. Some 200,000 Japanese were killed in two atomic bomb blasts in Hiroshima and Nagasaki in August 1945. A few years earlier in Nanking, the Japanese had killed an estimated 250,000 to 300,000 Chinese, mostly civilians. Total dead in World War II is estimated to be 60 million, with two-thirds of them civilians. Almost half a million civilians died in Vietnam during its two-decade civil war. So much for the civilizing influence of society across the years.

Recently an old Greenwich, Connecticut, friend asked when we might move back to "civilization." Caroline and I moved to Old Lyme from Greenwich twenty years ago. It got me thinking about civilization. My first reaction was to explain that I enjoyed the bucolic sense Old Lyme offers and especially our place on the marsh rivers near the mouth of the Connecticut. The contrast between standing on the catwalk watching the season's first ospreys circling lazily in the sky and competing with thirtysomethings driving SUVs almost the size of my first house for a parking spot on Greenwich Avenue made my response quite easy.

But civilization is not about the rural beauty of southeastern Connecticut, any more than it is about playing bumper cars in Greenwich. It is a state of mind; it is an ideal worth striving for. It is the freedom each of us has to pursue our dreams, to speak and assemble unafraid. It is living in a society based on laws, one that supports the concept of the greatest good for the greatest number. But, not unlike Stuart Little's quest, the search for the Holy Grail, or the pursuit of the pot at the end of a rainbow, it is an elusive and unreachable goal. It is an ideal that a civilized people will never give up. The bombs that went off near the

finish line of Boston's marathon do not indicate that we are uncivilized, but they do say that there are those among us who are. We have been involved in a war against terror for many years—even before 9/11. It is a war that will last decades, which means we must remain vigilant, even as we cannot allow such actions to disrupt our freedoms.

According to Wikipedia, the word *civilization*, derived from *civilis*, is also related to the Latin *civis*, meaning *citizen*, and *civitas*, meaning *city* or *city-state*. With that as a definition, the balance between Greenwich and Old Lyme would likely tip in favor of Greenwich. But the opposite of civility is rudeness, and certainly I encountered more rudeness in Greenwich than in Old Lyme, at least in daily random encounters.

Connecticut—She Loves Me, She Loves Me Not

September 12, 2014

A window opening onto fair meadows of hopefulness.

The Night Mirror, 1971
John Hollander (1929–2013)
Connecticut Poet Laureate (2007–2011)

PROFESSOR SEMIR ZEKI of University College London would not be surprised if I find myself both loving and hating the state in which I was born, and in which I have lived for fifty years. A study by the British biologist showed that some of the nervous circuits in the brain responsible for love are the same as those responsible for hate.

Connecticut has great beauty and plentiful resources, both of the natural and human kind. But in the past two decades its political leaders have adopted policies that have impeded economic growth and limited individual freedom.

Nevertheless, one could say the state is in my blood, as I have ancestors who were here 350 years ago. I was born here and have lived here most of my life. Young women in 1940, if they could, would often return to their mothers when they were about to give birth. That was especially true with a woman's first births. That decision must have seemed obvious when the alternative was a small farmhouse with no central heat during a cold New Hampshire winter. So my mother went back to her parents in Madison late that year, when eight months pregnant with me. Grace New Haven Hospital became my first home, for a week or so, when I was born at the end of January of 1941. A few years later, during the war, my mother returned home again with her horses, goats, and three children, while pregnant with a fourth. My father had been shipped overseas to fight the Nazis in Italy. We would live in Madison for about a year and a half.

Since we were married in 1964, Caroline and I have lived in Connecticut, other than our first year when I was still at college in New Hampshire. We have lived in four Connecticut towns—briefly in Glastonbury and Durham, and for almost a quarter of a century each in Greenwich and Old Lyme. It is a state I love. From the green fields and rolling hills of Litchfield County, to the rural farms in Windham County, to the 618 miles of coastline that stretch from Greenwich to Stonington, it is a state easy to embrace. Through the center of the state, passing through the capital of Hartford, descends the Connecticut, New England's longest and largest river. It takes its name from the Algonquin *quinnetukut*, which means "the long tidal river." The river runs 410 miles from just south of the Canadian border to its mouth. It empties into Long Island Sound, with Old Saybrook on the west bank and Old Lyme on the east. Its estuary, on which we now live, is filled with marsh islands and small creeks, and has been designated by the Nature Conservancy as one of the forty Last Great Places in the Western Hemisphere.

With a median household income of $65,753, Connecticut ranks

fourth-highest in the nation. The state has the most educated population in the country, with 36.2 percent having a bachelor's degree or higher. It has one of the highest concentrations of educational institutions in the country, with Yale, Trinity, Wesleyan, Connecticut College, and the US Coast Guard Academy within thirty-five miles of our home in Old Lyme. It is home to innumerable corporate executives. It has a thriving art academy in Old Lyme. The state is an important link between New York and Boston, with its highways (often bumper to bumper), rail, and air transport systems. From the south, it is the gateway to New England.

So it is sad that this state, so rich in resources and skills, should be doing so poorly by its citizens. Consider these numbers:

- The Department of Commerce ranked Connecticut 50 out of 50 states for annual economic growth in 2012.
- The American Legislative Council, for the same year, ranked Connecticut 46 for economic performance and 43 for economic outlook.
- *Barron's* states that Connecticut has the highest level of state debt and pension liabilities per taxpayer of any state in the union.
- In the past six years, the workforce shrank by 3,000.
- Median household income has declined by 4 percent since 2008.
- The Tax Foundation publishes a State Business Climate Index. On its list of the ten worst, Connecticut is prominently displayed. *Forbes*, slightly more generous, ranks the state 33 in overall business climate.
- Even before the financial meltdown, between 1996 and 2006 the number of small businesses operating in Connecticut declined by 2.2 percent.

Connecticut is a study in contrasts. It is home to some of America's richest individuals, but 10 percent of its residents live below the poverty level. Median family income ranges from $242,000 in Weston to

$32,000 in Hartford. The median value of its owner-occupied homes is 57 percent above the national average at $285,000, yet the amount of state debt per capita is the highest in the nation. Unemployment in the state is second-highest in New England. The State Business Tax Climate Index ranks the state among the ten worst in the nation. Yet in terms of "quality of life," another survey ranks the state second in the nation. Maintaining this split, the "business costs index" has the state three from the bottom. (Such dichotomies can be experienced in personal ways. The other day, as I ruefully pondered my September quarterly tax payment, a deer gracefully crossed the lawn!) A combination of repressive taxes and overregulation has created this situation. Every new rule imposed means one less arrow in our quiver of freedom. There is a yin-yang to Connecticut that causes people to love the state, yet want to move out. The "yang" seems to be winning. Over the past two decades, 300,000 more Connecticut residents have moved out than moved in.

As for us, our hearts being bigger than our heads, Caroline and I are likely to remain residents. It doesn't make much common or economic sense, but there is so much about the state we love: the stone walls that guard the back roads; the quiet, tree-lined streets with their colonial homes; the smell of the marshes that remind me of my grandparents' home in Madison; the book barns that I frequent; the beaches along Long Island Sound. We enjoy walking through the Duck River Cemetery in Old Lyme, where stones mark the graves of veterans from every war in which Americans have fought and died, from King Philip's War in 1676 to Vietnam in 1973. We appreciate the history and admire the men and women who came to this place with nothing but determination to carve from the land a living, a place where they could live in freedom. I wonder—would I have had the courage to leave a home, with city streets, shops, family, and friends, in order to make a new life in an unexplored wilderness? I don't know the answer, but since some of my ancestors did make that commitment, I feel an obligation to honor their pledge.

But I hope and I pray that those whom we have elected to run our government will have the common sense to allow this dream to continue. I worry, because I know that those whom we elected have promised more than can reasonably be provided, and that the cost of their largesse (our money) will have negative consequences: the dependency of the few on the production of the many is changing and becoming a dependency of the many on a productive few. That trend is one of the explanations for the widening income gap that troubles us all. More troubling, though, is the realization that once the dependent outnumber the productive, our democracy will cease.

In the meantime, however, we have this beautiful place. Whether one looks out on Sharon's hills or Putnam's farms, at office towers in Hartford or the cloisters of Yale's colleges, at former mills of fading brick in Middletown or at beautiful homes along the sound in Greenwich, or at the marshes before our house in Old Lyme, we have in Connecticut, as the poet John Hollander wrote, "a window opening onto fair / meadows of hopefulness." Let us hope it stays that way.

Partisan Politics

February 11, 2010

Divisions that now characterize the Senate were epitomized by the empty tables in the Senators' private dining room, a place where members of both parties used to break bread.

Senator Max Baucus
As quoted by David Herszenhorn
New York Times, December 24, 2009

"There's no beginning, never will be end."
It makes us nutty; hang the astral chimes.
The table's spread; come, let us dine, my friend.

"Quatrains," *The Spell of the Yukon*, 1907
Robert Service (1874–1958)

THIRTY-EIGHT YEARS AGO, during a period of great divisiveness, President Nixon gave a speech on the Vietnam War in which he said: "And so tonight—to you, the great silent majority of my fellow Americans—I ask for your support." Despite the fact that Nixon proved to be a crook and as polarizing a figure as ever occupied the White House, he was correct in his assessment that a lot of people at the time felt disenfranchised. Many feel the same way today. It in part explains the recent rise of the Tea Party movement.

On the right, the Republican Party has been hijacked by xenophobic religious zealots who feel that God is their copilot. On the left, supercilious coastal elites, emitting a sense of entitlement and spouting feel-good policies such as preventing climate change and cash-for-clunkers, have taken over the Democratic Party.

The results are loud and boisterous sidelines and an ever-enlarging, but mute, center, to which many of us belong; we also sense that there are few who represent us. Thomas Friedman recently compared the situation to a patient just out of intensive care, with all the doctors and nurses bickering: "Are you people crazy? . . . Aren't there any adults here?"

Partisanship by itself is neither disturbing nor unusual in the two-hundred-year-plus history of our republic. What makes some of us uncomfortable is the apparent lack of civility. Peggy Noonan, in *Patriotic Grace*, has written on the subject. The refusal to eat together, as Senator Baucus suggests in the quote above, is a visible manifestation of this attitude. Of course, the line between adamancy and blindly ignoring opposing arguments is diaphanous at best and invisible at worst.

The questions are: Is partisanship as bad as it ever has been? What was the genesis of today's partisanship? Is the lack of civility damaging to our democracy?

Historical Review

Politics and the media have always been closely intertwined. Pamphleteers were the forefathers of today's bloggers. George Orwell, in *British Pamphleteers*, described their role: "They had the complete freedom of expression to be scurrilous, abusive, and seditious; or, on the other hand, to be more detailed, serious, and 'highbrow' than is possible in a newspaper or in most kinds of periodicals." According to Bernard Bailyn, writing in *The Ideological Origins of the American Revolution*, the purpose of pamphleteers was "to free the individual from the oppressive misuse of power, from the tyranny of the state." The comments are applicable to today's bloggers, who fear the seizure of power by Washington. Marcus Daniel, in his book *Scandal and Civility*, writes: "Far from being an age of classical virtue and republican self-restraint, political life in pre-revolutionary United States was tempestuous, fiercely partisan, and highly personal."

Thomas Paine, author of perhaps the most famous pamphlet of that time, *Common Sense*, in a July 1796 letter to George Washington called him a "cold Hermaphrodite"—a symbolic slap at a man who despite being the "father of his country" fathered no children; the insult is proof that not even the most revered man in the newly established United States was above being slandered.

Congress in those early days witnessed brawls and fistfights. On the morning of February 15, 1798, Federalist representative Roger Griswold of Connecticut strode across the floor of the House and with his hickory walking stick struck Vermont Republican Matthew Lyon. The attack was not a random act of violence. A couple of weeks earlier, Lyon had insulted Griswold and spat in his face.

Partisanship, no doubt, was at its most extreme at the time of the Civil War. In 1856, Representative Preston Brooks of South Carolina, furious at the North's interference with the South's way of life, beat Senator Charles Sumner of Massachusetts unconscious with a gold-topped cane. The war itself saw a number of politicians enlist. Jefferson Davis, elected President of the Confederacy, had been a Mississippi senator. Congressmen Benjamin Franklin Butler of New Hampshire, Francis Blair, Jr. of Missouri, John Logan of Illinois, and Daniel Sickles of New York, among others, served as generals in the Union Army. Representatives William Barksdale of Mississippi and Milledge Bonham of South Carolina became generals in the Army of the Confederacy. Two brothers (both politicians) from Kentucky, Thomas Leonidas Crittenden and George Bibb Crittenden, served as generals in opposing armies. John C. Breckinridge of Kentucky had served as vice president under James Buchanan and then joined the Confederacy as a general.

In the years following the Civil War, years that saw a great increase in immigration, congressional partisanship was abetted by constituents growing in numbers, knowledge, demands, and diversity. Newspapers proliferated during the first 175 years of our history, providing outlets for partisan feelings. Noah Webster, better known for his dictionary, established America's first daily newspaper in 1793 in New York, the *American Minerva* (later the *Commercial Advertiser*). While seven newspapers dominated the city of New York in the late nineteenth century, every political view and every ethnic group had its own paper or sheet. Cities like New York had papers in every borough, representing the hundred or more languages that were spoken throughout the city. What now constitutes New York City had a population of 60,000 in 1800. By 1900 that number mushroomed to 3.4 million, all speaking with individual voices and all demanding representation.

The New York Press coined the term *yellow journalism* in 1897, a phrase that described so-called down-market papers like Joseph Pulitzer's *New York World* and William Randolph Hearst's *New York Journal*. At the end of the nineteenth century, muckrakers like Ida Tarbell—subsequent to pamphleteers and antecedent to today's bloggers—rallied populist ire against big business and the trusts that operated them. President Theodore Roosevelt adopted populism as his own, becoming infamous as the "Trust Buster."

Partisanship, encouraged by a spirited and opinionated press, was very much a part of the political landscape into the first half of the twentieth century.

Genesis of Today's Partisanship

Following the end of the Depression and the Second World War, consolidation began to limit the number of newspapers—thereby limiting the expression of a multiplicity of opinions. At the same time, network television came to dominate the evening news and, while each broadcaster had his own style, opinions were muted and tended to be centrist. The result was a (false, in my opinion) sense of a nation in unison. There were obvious and notorious exceptions to this feeling of camaraderie, the McCarthy hearings in the early 1950s being, perhaps, the best example. Two decades after the end of World War II, in the mid-1960s, divisiveness reappeared in the antiwar movement as Vietnam came to dominate the news. However, those twenty years—1945 to 1965—of relative calm were the decades when I and my generation grew up, and they influenced the way we see things. Most of the country had united behind the war to defeat Hitler and Hirohito in 1941.

That sense of a united people was particularly strong during the Eisenhower years.

Eisenhower, a grandfatherly figure, known for his ability to work with and reconcile the egos of generals ranging from Patton to Montgomery, was the perfect person to bring calm to a nation that had undergone a decade and a half of depression and war. The 1950s were a time of renewed economic growth and the emergence of the United States as the leader of the free world.

Vietnam brought that period of serenity to an end. Woodstock and the Democratic convention in Chicago in 1968, for example, were events we will always remember. Through it all—Vietnam, Kent State, Nixon's resignation—Walter Cronkite and Eric Sevareid on CBS and Chet Huntley and David Brinkley on NBC kept their cool and, staying centrist, kept us informed. Personal opinion took a backseat to news, and the country survived what could have been a real challenge to its stability.

This period of reasonableness on the part of the press, reflected in politicians who, despite differences, at least were civil to one another, was an anomaly in American political history. Ethnic differences vanished into the melting pot that was America, so many local papers failed. Intense competition put others like the *New York Herald Tribune* out of business. What we got was news without the edge we get today from CNN or Fox.

That began to change about 1980. CNN, founded by Ted Turner, became one of the first cable news channels, with David Walker and Lois Hart (a husband-wife team) as anchors. As time went on, and perhaps in response to the Reagan years, their programming increasingly moved to the left. In 1996 Rupert Murdoch, with Roger Ailes as CEO and Brit Hume as anchor, launched Fox News with 17 million cable subscribers to counter the influence of CNN. Today Fox News serves more than 100 million people and is the most-watched news program in America. In recent years, the tone of both channels has become more strident, with Bill O'Reilly and Glenn Beck at Fox being offset by Chris Matthews and Keith Olbermann of MSNBC, and Jack Cafferty and Wolf Blitzer at CNN.

The recent intensification of partisanship, though, can be partially attributed to the plethora of blogs. The term *weblog* was coined in 1997 by Jorn Barger, and the first blogs were up and running by 1999. Today it is estimated that worldwide there are 300 million blogs, growing at the rate of fifty every half second, or about 60 million a year. One can see that, with seven billion people on the planet, in a few decades there could be one per person. In that they are simple and provide quick means for individuals to express their opinions, they resemble the pamphlets of the Revolutionary War period, multiplied by millions. The Tea Parties of last summer were greatly aided by bloggers, and the ease and ubiquitous nature of the Internet.

In many respects the vitriol of bloggers, forerunners and fomenters of political partisanship, is a reaction to politicians who increasingly are divorced from the people they purportedly represent. Gerrymandering has created congressional districts that are no longer competitive, and so provide lifelong sinecures for members of Congress, at least until the officeholder dies or goes to jail. It takes millions of dollars to finance a campaign today for a new candidate, money that too often comes from lobbyists and other special interest groups. However, the Internet has provided the ability to raise millions of dollars for grassroots campaigns.

Are Partisanship and a Lack of Civility Damaging Over the Longer Term?

Edmund S. Morgan[3], professor emeritus at Yale University, has described representational government as a fiction—a fiction because it is impossible to represent every citizen's view. Those of us who grew up in small towns know and appreciate real representative government. Every citizen is invited and encouraged to attend town hall meetings.

---

3. Edmund Sears Morgan was an American historian. An authority on American colonial history, he died in 2013.

Each voter has his say. As our country has grown, we have moved further from that ideal. With 435 House members[4] and a hundred senators, our legislators must perform a balancing act between the needs of their constituents and those of the nation. It is a conflict that is as old as the nation and divided Federalists, like John Adams, and early Republicans, like Thomas Jefferson. Our bicameral legislature came about in part as a compromise between the Federalists and the anti-Federalists. In contrast to 1789 when each representative represented 60,000 citizens, today each of the 435 House members represents about 700,000 people—an obviously increasingly fictionalized version of a representative form of government, to borrow the words of Professor Morgan. While the system has served us well, there is a growing sense that people are feeling increasingly disenfranchised.

A possible future problem will be finding attractive candidates to run for public office. The ubiquity of YouTube, Facebook, chat rooms, IM, e-mail, etc., has made every person's life an open book. The questions will become: Who will permit (not to mention, who can afford to have) their past so closely scrutinized? Will the media play the role of spoiler or, worse, accomplice? As a people, do we run the risk of losing our democracy, especially in a commercially competitive world?

China, still a communist dictatorship but with an estimated 80,000 protests a year, has adopted censorship, through limiting Internet access, to assert control. But history suggests that as the wealth and education of a people grow, so does the desire to think and act freely. Either the heavy foot of government will come down, or democracy, with all its inefficiencies, will assert itself.

Marshall McLuhan had it wrong. The medium is *not* the message; at least it isn't any longer. The message is the message. Politicians would be wise to listen to the rumblings of Americans, speaking in millions of voices, who are upset with their leaders and the direction they fear the major parties are taking the country. America, accord-

---

4. The number of House members was fixed in 1911, at a time when the population was about 93 million, less than a third of what it is today.

ing to most polls, is a center-right country, much as it has been for decades. The problem is that vocal extremists have hijacked the two parties. And neither one speaks to the desires, concerns, and fears of those millions who have banded together to form Tea Parties—a movement David Brooks alleges is bigger than either of the two major parties. On the left, the state has been elevated above the individual. The state, to millions of Americans, is not the end; it is a means to an end—the end being an individual free to make choices, to succeed or fail, to express his or her opinions. Both parties seem focused on their own narrow agendas—Democrats view the electorate as children in need of care and direction; Republicans have a singular focus on faith-based programs, with little tolerance for those who disagree with them. Neither party seems conscious that it is the antics of Washington and the establishment and the endangerment of individual rights that worry people, and that listening to Nancy Pelosi do battle with John Boehner is wearing and boring. Lost in the noise is what is most important to our future—economics and a civil debate as to which path we should travel.

"Scandal and incivility," writes Marcus Daniel in *Scandal and Civility,* "were closely linked to the creation of a more democratic and participating political culture." So perhaps the discord we are now witnessing is not such a bad thing. What is important is how we and government adjust. Thomas Jefferson spoke of the desirability of a revolution every generation. While that seems extreme, the concept may not be. Our founders laid down specific broad principles, but they also allowed room for expansion.

One answer, it seems to me, is term limits. No matter what one may think of her politics, Sarah Palin made a wise statement during her campaign in 2008 when she said she did not see herself as part of a "permanent government." Government does have permanent workers, hundreds of thousands of them, the staff that keeps the bearings of politics oiled, but elected officials were never supposed to be in that position. We are breeding a class of people whose children inherit their parents' vocation. Early on the Adams family was prominent, but today politics is becoming more of a family business. Examples include the Bush, Kennedy, and Gore families. In 2000, two sons of prominent politicians (Bush and Gore) ran for president. Chris Dodd of Connecticut followed his father to the Senate. Speaker of the House Nancy Pelosi's father, Thomas D'Alesandro, was mayor of Baltimore and a House representative. Harry Reid's son is running for governor of Nevada. When Joe Biden gave up his Senate seat to become vice president, the word was that it was being held for his son, Beau. Is that right? Ted Kennedy's seat in the Senate has been referred to as Senator Kennedy's seat. It is not. It is the people of Massachusetts' seat, as newly elected Senator Scott Brown so eloquently put it. The cost to mount a campaign to unseat a House or Senate member in a "safe" district is becoming so high that only very rich people can run. Again, is that democracy? The potential of creating an aristocracy of political leaders worried the founding fathers—the possibility that our leaders would increasingly become divorced from working men and women. Shouldn't this concern us?[5]

The time of crisis we experienced in the fall of 2008, when our financial system came perilously close to collapse, created an environment in which extremists proliferate. In saving the system, government saved the banks, a necessary though now, with the benefit of time and hindsight, increasingly unpopular decision. In response, populism has risen in both parties, a form of expression that makes its case by demonizing the opposition. Republicans like Sarah Palin have set "real" Americans—those in small-town Middle America—against cultural elites along the two coasts. Democrats, like the president in recent speeches, are doing the same thing, pitting Main Street against Wall Street.

---

5. Beau Biden chose not to seek his father's seat; he died in 2015. The Senate seat once held by Ted Kennedy was won by Scott Brown, a Republican, in an indication that independents are a strong force even in Massachusetts, the bluest of the blue states.

One can argue that today's partisanship reflects two very different views of the future: on the left, there is a strong sense that government is the answer; on the right, there is conviction that the answer lies with private enterprise. The stakes are high. In a sense, it is Keynes versus Schumpeter—demand-side economics versus supply-side.

The credit crisis has been resolved and the economy is improving. But unemployment remains high and nobody expects this year's growth to be particularly robust. The only sector of the economy experiencing employment growth is government. That is to be expected during recession, but the risk is that Congress does what it is good at—spending money, and that they have been doing, taking federal debt to $12.3 trillion, just below the debt ceiling. (The debt ceiling was raised to $14.3 trillion on January 28 to accommodate the $3.8 trillion current-year budget.) Federal debt, as a percent of GDP, is at the highest level since World War II. All of this provides fodder to bloggers and populists within our government, exacerbating partisanship in Washington.

The president has noted the unfortunate influence of money in our campaigns and in Washington, and I agree, there is too much money chasing political influence. But the answer lies not in imposing artificial limits, but in allowing full disclosure of all moneys paid to candidates and making that information readily available for all to see and read. And it lies in reducing the power and influence of congressional members, an effect that can be best achieved through the imposition of term limits, permitting a citizens' government and then allowing those who have served to return to their homes and to real jobs with all the ups and downs experienced by their constituents.

Political partisanship is inextricably tied to the media (including bloggers and the Internet), which fans the embers of extremism. While we cannot, democratically, stop the presses, we can certainly learn to be more civil.

Politicians can be both partisan and civil. But today partisanship is omnipresent and civility is absent. Civility is a function of culture. The

country has been through far more difficult periods than the one we are now facing. There is no reason why civility cannot return (as Robert Service wrote in "Quatrains," quoted above: "Come, let us dine, my friend.") But restoring civility will require changing attitudes among parents, teachers, and political leaders. The examples they set provide the framework for change. Partisanship, in my opinion, is fine, as long as it is conducted within reasonable bounds; it has a long history in our country and it keeps everybody on edge. But keep it civil.

BOOKS AND OTHER INTERESTS

THIS SECTION HAS THE FEWEST ESSAYS, but that is no reflection on its importance. Early in our marriage, Caroline and I lived in a small town in central Connecticut, Durham. Two houses down the street was a retired couple. He was British and had recently retired from the *Nation*, for which he wrote for many years. In retirement, he started a used-book business. Basically he was charged with searching for books for college libraries, but in his wanderings he ended up buying collections from individuals.

A few years later, one of my younger brothers opened a bookstore in Peterborough where we had grown up. The store, under Willard's wise and keen charge, has been successful beyond his dreams.

Both events helped nourish my latent interest in books, and two essays on the subject constitute half of this section. The other two—one on violins and the other on laughter—are unrelated, but seem to fit neatly here.

In Defense of Books—Real Books
May 28, 2009

The person, be it gentleman or lady, who has not pleasure
in a good novel, must be intolerably stupid.

Jane Austen (1775–1817)

Those of you who have seen my house in Connecticut or my apartment in New York know my love of books. They dominate my apartment, and the shelves in Connecticut are overflowing. Despite this apparent disorder, as long as no one touches anything, I can usually find what I am looking for.

My thoughts on this subject surfaced upon receipt of my Kindle 2. It had been recommended by two friends who are great readers and book lovers. One travels a good deal and says it has reduced the problem of what book to take with him. The second told me that his reading had fallen off because of eye problems. The Kindle, with its adjustable font, rekindled his interest.

The *Random House Dictionary* defines a book as "a written work of fiction or nonfiction, usually on sheets of paper fastened or bound together within covers." According to the fifteenth edition of the *Encyclopedia Britannica*, a book is an "instrument of communication which employs the use of writing or symbols to convey meaning in a publication for *tangible* circulation." With a precision that baffles me, but sounding appropriately politically correct, UNESCO defines a book as a "nonperiodical printed publication of at least forty-nine pages excluding covers." Regardless, we all know what a book is when we see one, unless it is embedded on a microchip.

The coming of electronic books raises questions, not only for readers but also for those in the business. Will the advent of the electronic book place bookstores—stores already under pressure from recession and Amazon—in further jeopardy? Nobody knows the answer, but my brother Willard, who founded, owns, and operates The Toadstool (a chain of three bookstores in southern New Hampshire), expresses some concern. While his sales continue reasonably robust, he views this as the first real threat in his thirty-seven years in the business. According to Willard, electronic books appeal principally to those who read paperback novels, who have little interest in sharing what they read, and who have no intention to build a library; nevertheless, their proliferation, he suspects, will impact sales. Electronic readers provide previews of books and they allow the reader to purchase titles for about 30 to 40 percent of the cost of a hardcover. Longer term, Willard worries that the Kindle and similar electronic book readers will not be good for booksellers, publishers, or writers. Copyright problems will pursue writers and publishers alike, as electronic thieves proliferate. Unlike music, digitized books are generally consumed once, and the question as to who will absorb the reduced prices remains unanswered. Also unknown is whether electronic books will increase overall sales of an author's work. Units may well increase, but will revenues?

Steven Johnson and Yukari Kane, in the April 20 issue of the *Wall Street Journal*, wrote, as regards electronic books: "Readers will have the option to purchase a chapter for ninety-nine cents, the same way they buy an individual song on iTunes. The marketplace will start to produce modular books that can be intelligibly split into stand-alone chapters." That would suggest a return to the practices of the nineteenth century when authors like Charles Dickens, James Fenimore Cooper, Wilkie Collins, Edward Everett Hale, Sir Arthur Conan Doyle, and others had their stories serialized in weekly magazines.

While I find the Kindle useful on trips and easy to carry (and even easier for downloading a novel if one is caught short), it is not wholly satisfying. I like the feel and look of real books. Real books satisfy three of the five senses—sight, feel, and smell.

At Home with Books is a coffee-table book by Estelle Ellis, Caroline Seebohm, and Christopher Simon Sykes. The three authors wrote, "Book-centered homes are described as nurturing, a comfort zone, an escape hatch, a place to retreat to for . . . thinking . . . regenerating spirit and ideas." They also state that "libraries, perhaps more than any other room in the house, express the personality of the owner."

Thomas Wright, in his recent biography of Oscar Wilde, *Built of Books,* describes Wilde's library: "The library served him as a retreat from the rest of the house; it was a symbol of his personal history, as its contents bore witness to the various stages of his life." The title of Anthony Powell's 1971 novel *Books Do Furnish a Room* is my idea of ideal interior decorating. Walking into a room shelved with books, especially a personal library, is a delight. Book covers, whether leather or cloth, are attractive and incite curiosity. A peculiar smell, a combination of leather bindings mixed with the smell of paper and shelves and collected dust, is a musty scent familiar to all book lovers. The sight of colorful dust jackets and stately rows of enriched leather bindings encourage one to select a volume and peruse it for familiar passages or search for something new. A collection of books, amassed over many years, recalls for the owner past days and provides for the visitor insight into the owner.

Nassim Taleb begins *The Black Swan* with a quote from Italian medievalist and mystery writer Umberto Eco about his personal library, a library containing thirty thousand volumes. Mr. Eco is quoted as saying, "A private library is not an ego-boosting appendage but a research tool. Read books are far less valuable than unread ones . . . and the growing numbers of unread books look at you menacingly."

My own library is relatively small—perhaps four thousand volumes, of which about half are actually in my library. The rest are scattered through other rooms and my New York apartment. A library is a special place, a shrine to years of gathering and collecting. I sit in my library and look about: three shelves devoted to genealogy; six to works on finance; three to town histories; two shelves of dictionaries; four dedicated to the Civil War; fifteen shelves holding the works of P. G. Wodehouse; three shelves of poetry; five of leather-bound classics—Dickens, Kipling, Austen, Brontë, Leigh Hunt, George DuMaurier, and Oliver Wendell Holmes—and three of presentation or signed works of fiction. A hidden cupboard houses an eclectic collection of special books—many of little monetary value, but special to me. In the cabinets below the open shelves resides a potpourri of fiction and nonfiction, including two dozen books about the Tenth Mountain Division with whom my father served during WWII and another couple of dozen books devoted to the Holocaust, an event I remember my father saying, after returning from Italy, we must never forget. On the floor lie dozens of other books, homeless for the moment, but ones I cannot bear to give up. In other rooms on other shelves lie histories of our country from the Revolutionary War through the present, a few hundred mysteries, and a wealth of other fiction, history, biography, letters, autobiographies, and essays. I am told that all these books could be housed on three or four Kindles, reducing space consumed from substantial to minimal. Would I get the same deep satisfaction and sense of wonder gazing at three electronic readers that I get when my eyes sweep across the myriad titles in their colorful bindings? I don't think so.

Electronic books do not provide the owner the connection to the past that shelves of books do. Anne Fadiman, in *Ex Libris*, expresses the sentiment: "What I consider the heart of reading: not whether we wish to purchase a new book but how we maintain our connections with our old books, the ones we have lived with for years, the ones whose texture and colors and smells have become as familiar to us as our children's skin."

Books have long been feared by dictators and other repressive heads of state, as the ideas books generate are often at odds with their policies. We should keep in mind that Hitler, Stalin, and Mussolini strode the world stage a mere seventy years ago—not long in the history of man and culture. We must appreciate what we have; we should never assume the continuity of anything valued. Books are a reminder of the fragility of our existence, the diversity of our cultures, and the hours spent writing in order to educate and entertain.

Real books allow for grazing. We all have many examples of such books. A few of mine include: *Curiosities of Literature* by John Sutherland; *The Oxford Book of Satirical Verse,* edited by Geoffrey Grigson; *A Gentle Madness* by Nicholas Basbanes, a book that describes my affliction; and, of course, *The Elements of Style* by William Strunk and E. B. White. I cannot imagine using my Kindle for such meanderings.

There is surely a place in our wide and diverse world for electronic books; I would hope they stimulate reading, as paperbacks have, and, in doing so, encourage the purchase of their real cousins so that more libraries will be built to contain the books one loves. Books provide busy people the opportunity to "smell the flowers." They provide an outlet for creative people to earn a living doing what they love. They have given people like me the chance to live out the passion of amassing books—at a rate faster than I can read them; but, like good friends, I know they will be there when I need them.

Andrew Lang, the nineteenth-century author of a series of fairy tale books, begins his "Ballade of His Books":

> *Here stand my books, line upon line,*
> *They reach the roof, and row by row*
> *They speak of faded tastes of mine,*
> *And things I did, but do not, know.*

I rest my case.

Reading for Pleasure and Knowledge

December 22, 2011

*A capacity and taste for reading gives access
to whatever has already been discovered by others.*

Abraham Lincoln (1809–1865)

I Can Read with My Eyes Shut! (1978)

Dr. Seuss (Theodor Seuss Geisel, 1904–1991)

FROM TIME TO TIME I GET ASKED about the books I read. There is nothing remarkable in the list. Several friends read a lot more and a few, less. For the past ten years, I have kept tabs on the books I have read, largely as a reminder, for age has reduced my ability to retain.

Books have always been important to me. My habit is to buy them faster than I can read them. While I have both a Kindle and an iPad, and have read books on both devices, I prefer real books. My library is eclectic, with books ranging from current fiction to town histories, from the classics to favorite literature from childhood. One of my favorite things about books is that they transport you from wherever

you are to a different place in another time. While others would rather spend leisure hours watching sports or favorite TV shows, I prefer to immerse myself in a period of history or a fictional character.

Books I have read over the past two years include three classics—reminders that, no matter how creative we have become or how sophisticated we are, the art of writing knows no time: *David Copperfield* by Charles Dickens, *Anna Karenina* by Leo Tolstoi, and Anthony Trollope's *Barchester Towers* demonstrate that time has not damped the music of words written a hundred fifty years ago. Generally these are books we read in school or in college—too early in our lives to fully appreciate their beauty and their wisdom. They are worth rereading today. In my opinion, *Anna Karenina* is the best novel ever published.

For almost forty years I have collected the works of P. G. Wodehouse, the British humorist known among aficionados as "the Master" and who was described by Hilaire Belloc as the best prose writer of his age; so I always read a couple of his. *The Code of the Woosters*, written in 1938 when he was at the peak of his formidable talents, is my favorite. Lee Childs, Charles Todd (a mother-son team), and Jacqueline Winspear write diverting, fast-reading mysteries. Amor Towles wrote an extraordinary first novel, *Rules of Civility*, a story involving four friends that takes place in New York City throughout the year

1938. *The Wall Street Journal* recently named the book one of the top ten novels of 2011. Not only is Amor a beautiful writer, but he is an articulate speaker, as we discovered when we recently hosted a lunch for him. And my daughter-in-law Beatriz Chantrill Williams will have her first novel, *Overseas,* published by Putnam in May 2012. I had the pleasure of reading an advance copy of the manuscript a few months ago and found it a great read. Julian and Kate are memorable characters who transcend two time periods (the trenches on the Western Front during World War I and the hedge fund world of modern day New York). I will leave it to the reader to see how she makes this surreal leap; suffice it to say that she does so in a totally credible fashion.

In terms of nonfiction, my interests lie principally in history. *American* Heroes by Edmund Morgan, Richard Brookhiser's *James Madison,* and Ron Chernow's *Washington* covered the Revolutionary War period. Adam Hochschild's tale of the incredible bravery of antiwar pacifists during World War I, *To End All Wars,* is as moving and powerful as anything I have read. *A Journey: My Political Life* by Tony Blair was fascinating to read alongside George W. Bush's *Decision Points,* particularly regarding the events leading up to the Iraq invasion—how they both arrived at the same decision, but from different perspectives. Blair's more analytical mind could be contrasted with Bush's instinctive judgments. There were other fascinating books. David Reynolds's *Mightier Than the Sword* tells the story of Harriet Beecher Stowe writing *Uncle Tom's Cabin.* Lincoln, on meeting the author in 1862, allegedly said: "So you are the little woman who wrote the book that started this great war." Stacy Schiff's *Cleopatra* carries the reader back two thousand years. I still find it hard to believe that the main street in Alexandria, at the time of Cleopatra, was as wide as Park Avenue in New York today, and that the sides of the street were designed so that sewage could be carried off. It is humbling to realize that at the time there was no civilization in Northern Europe, and it would be almost 1,500 years before America would be "discovered."

Other fiction titles that I particularly enjoyed were Jacques Chessex's powerful tale of the Nazi influence in wartime Switzerland, *A Jew Must Die*, and Mario Vargas Llosa's *Feast of the Goat*, which tells the story of the brutality of Trujillo's reign in the Dominican Republic.

Who could not be amazed and moved by Laura Hillenbrand's story of survival in the Pacific and Japanese prison camps in *Unbroken*, or learn something about the financial crisis we continue to live through in reading George Melloan's *The Great Money Binge* or Michael Lewis's very readable *Boomerang*? Mitch Daniels's *Keeping the Republic* is the best thing I have read on how to extricate ourselves from what seems to be an intractable political morass.

As the quote from Lincoln at the top of this essay makes clear, reading is not only about enjoyment, it is about learning. There is an almost infinite amount of knowledge in the world of books, which is available to all for a reasonable price. And, as the title of Dr. Seuss's book makes clear, reading allows one to use one's imagination, a luxury in today's world where images from televisions, computers, and smartphones dance continuously before our eyes.

The Violin: Perfection Found Early

February 22, 2011

The violin, as we know it, is the most perfect development
of the large number of instruments played with a bow.

The Musical Times, May 1, 1888

Perfection is attained by slow degrees; it requires the hand of time.

Voltaire (1694–1778)

NOT HAVING MUCH OF A MUSIC SENSE, so shutting my eyes and enjoying the sensation, I was sitting recently in Old Lyme's First Congregational Church, the venue for Musical Masterworks, letting my mind wander. Two violinists were playing Dmitri Shostakovich's *Duets for Two Violins with Piano*. Not quite daydreaming, I had the thought that we live in a time when technology has radically changed our lives, for better and for worse, but mostly for better. Skis, clothes, tennis racquets, cars, TVs, telephones, drugs, music synthesizers, golf clubs—myriad products that we use every day have been improved thanks to advances in technology and the use of new materials, be they composites or rare-earth minerals. Yet a violin made by Antonio Stradivari in 1710, from material still available today, has never been improved upon. Why?

The nave of the church, which was rebuilt in 1909 with the aid of artists from the Old Lyme art colony, achieves almost perfect acoustics. Musical Masterworks is a series of five chamber music concerts that have been held here every year for the last twenty. The series was begun with Charles Wadsworth, the founding director of the Chamber Music Society of Lincoln Center, as artistic director. Two years ago Edward Arron, the artistic director for the Metropolitan Museum Artists in Concert, succeeded him. The artists come from around the world and have included this season Yosuke Kawasaki and Catherine

Cho (violins), Marya Martin (flute), Andrew Armstrong (piano), and Randall Scarlata (baritone).

Antonio Stradivari was likely born in Cremona in 1644. Around the age of thirteen he was apprenticed to luthier Niccolò Amati, grandson of Andrea Amati, the earliest maker of the violin as we know it today. Because Stradivari inscribed his violins with Latin slogans, they became known as Antonius Stradivarius violins. Today those instruments made during what was considered his "golden" period, between 1700 and 1720, command prices in the millions of dollars. The highest price paid at a public auction for a Stradivarius was $3,544,000 at Christie's in New York on May 15, 2006. It is estimated that instruments have sold for higher prices in private sales.

While a Stradivarius is generally considered the best violin ever made, there are have been blind tests, conducted between 1827 and the present, that question that conclusion—but in none of those tests has the sound quality of a Stradivarius ever been found wanting. Wikipedia suggests that while the techniques used in their construction have long been debated, it is known that Stradivari experimented with sizes. The woods used are known: spruce for the harmonic top, willow for the internal parts, and maple for the back, strip, and neck. All the wood, which was stored in Venice in and under water before being used, was treated with several types of minerals; the varnish comprised a mix of natural products. There are theories that the wood used was denser than that generally available today, due to the stunted growth of trees, a function of the Little Ice Age, which lasted from the mid-seventeenth to the mid-eighteenth century.

Whatever a violin's origin, in talented hands the result can be mesmerizing: the notes that evening flowed, somberly in the Prelude, cheerfully in the Gavotte, and the Waltz made the listener believe he/she was in mid-nineteenth-century Vienna.

However, given my lack of musical sophistication, my attendance at these concerts is somewhat akin to a nine-year-old being taken to see Shakespeare in the Park. It's easy to become distracted. I sit there and let the music sweep over me. I marvel at the composers and consider their genius, as writing music of this sort must be like writing a play, only far more complicated. Each instrument is played according to the specific demands of its individual script, sometimes in tune with the other instruments and at other times alone, or in opposition. The composer, faced with an empty sheet of paper, must write the music for each instrument; he must be able to hear the tune in his mind, the sound and tune from each instrument, and how they blend into a cohesive whole. The composer's genius is beyond my comprehension.

We live in an age when meetings on Facebook constitute a relationship and when twittering, IM, and YouTube have replaced person-to-person dialogue. Listening to Ms. Catherine Cho and Ms. Kyung Sun Lee, their bows moving rhythmically across the strings, producing sounds that can only be described as heavenly, I bask in the wonder that technology, which has altered our lives in so many ways, has been unable to improve upon an instrument made three hundred years ago in the ancient city of Cremona. And I smile.

Laughter, the Medicine That Works

January 18, 2011

I was irrevocably betrothed to laughter, the sound of which always seemed to me the most exciting civilized music in the world.

Peter Ustinov (1921–2004)

APART FROM THE SENSUALITY of cruising Cappuccino at day's start or flying down Born Free at day's end, or the adrenaline rush one gets from attacking a groomed Blue Ox in between, what I always remember best of my too-few days in Vail is the laughing—on the slopes, at lunch, and at dinner. Laughter serves as a release after an exciting, nerve-tingling run down Riva Ridge; it allows my longtime skiing companions and I to become easily reacquainted after months of absence.

Who can read great lines from P. G. Wodehouse without at least cracking a smile? "I could see that, if not actually disgruntled, he was far from gruntled." Or, "She looked as if she had been poured into her clothes and forgotten to say 'when.'" I am a member of a small group in New York, all aficionados of Wodehouse, called the Drones. We meet irregularly for dinner. In our youth we would toss rolls around the table—beaning the bald guy across and two seats down the table with a crusted roll when he looked away was a measure of sophistication, which caused raucous laughter from the rest. Our hands and arms have become stilled (with age?); nevertheless, our almost constant laughter still causes more sober diners to regard our childish antics with dismay.

An old Yiddish proverb says, "What soap is to the body, laughter is to the soul." But laughter may also have medicinal benefits. Medical experts claim it reduces muscle tension and distracts attention from pain—both emotional and physical. Not only does laughter act as a distraction, it stimulates the release of endorphins, the body's natural

painkillers. Doctors say the act of laughing is known to lower blood pressure, reduce stress hormones, and increase muscle flexion.

For most of my forty-four years on Wall Street, trading desks were the creative hot spots for jokes, especially (and morbidly) those dealing with tragic events. The jokes were never meant to be demeaning or disrespectful; they were simply means of relieving tension. Traders thrive on intensity. A poorly executed trade can mean the difference between a profit and a loss involving hundreds of thousands or even millions of dollars. Stress is often followed by laughter.

"Humor is one of the most serious tools we have for dealing with impossible situations"; so once wrote Erica Jong. In 1976, Norman Cousins published the first chapter of his book *Anatomy of an Illness* in the *New England Journal of Medicine*. He had been diagnosed a dozen years earlier with ankylosing spondylitis, an acute inflammation of the spine, and had been given only a few months to live. He left the hospital, checked into a hotel, took megadoses of vitamin C, and turned the TV to whatever humorous programs he could find. He discovered that ten minutes of boisterous laughter resulted in at least two hours of uninterrupted, pain-free sleep. He continued the routine until he recovered.

We live during a serious time. Radical Islamic terrorists attacked our country ten years ago. We are finally exiting the most severe economic collapse in eighty years. A gun-toting maniac just killed six people in Tucson and wounded a US representative. Every day in America, about eighty people are shot dead—some twenty-nine thousand every year. Does laughter seem too cavalier for dealing with today's problems? Do expressions of humor just seem callous and unfeeling? Violent Islamic protests broke out after the Danish newspaper *Jyllands-Posten* published a dozen editorial cartoons depicting the Islamic prophet Mohammad. Prime Minister Anders Fogh Rasmussen called the subsequent response (in which more than a hundred people were killed in locations around the world) Denmark's worst international crisis since World War II.

Yet the ability to laugh at oneself is critical in all situations. The Revolutionary War period in America was a trying time, and we don't often think of the founding fathers laughing their way through Philadelphia in 1776. The founders had put both their fortunes and their lives on the line when they broke with the crown. However, they were not without a sense of humor. Benjamin Franklin once suggested sending rattlesnakes to England in response to them sending convicted criminals to America. George Washington, who is generally portrayed as a stern icon, in 1755 wrote his brother John (in words that anticipated by 150 years similar remarks from one of the nation's greatest humorists, Mark Twain): "As I have heard since my arrival at this place a circumstantial account of my death and dying speech, I take this opportunity of . . . contradicting the first, and assuring you I have yet to compose the latter."

In our country, it has generally been those presidents with a good sense of humor—Lincoln, Roosevelt, and Reagan—with whom most of us feel the greatest identification. Others like Nixon and Carter, though perhaps possessing humor, never used it. It is a lesson presidents should learn.

Laughter is spontaneous. Shortly after I met my wife, she and I, along with her roommate, Posy, and Posy's boyfriend, Ed, were having drinks at the Eliot Lounge on the corner of Massachusetts and Commonwealth Avenues in Boston. Something that I can no longer recall caused Caroline to break out in paroxysms of laughter. Her contagious laugh was echoed by another young woman, who remained hidden from us in that darkened room. When one paused for breath, the other leapt into the breach. The effect was not unlike the mournful tone of taps reverberating off distant hills from a second, unseen bugler.

Laughter is not learned; it is instinctive. "Infants will laugh almost from birth," says well-known psychologist Steve Wilson, who refers to himself as a "joyologist." Jokes may help, but are not critical to laughter. Mr. Wilson points out that preschoolers laugh on average four hundred times a day, while adults laugh fewer than fifteen times. I have long felt that children are there to teach us; in this regard they can. Humor is equalizing; it admonishes the pretentious and lifts the depressed. "Laugh, and the world laughs with you; weep, and you weep alone"[6] is an old but true adage.

---

6 From the poem "Solitude" by Ella Wheeler Wilcox.

FAMILY AND FRIENDS

A YEAR AGO, BAUHAN PUBLISHED A BOOK of my essays, *One Man's Family: Growing Up in Peterborough and Other Stories.* This section includes more stories of family and friends (and one about a dog), but drawn from the years after I left Peterborough.

Family and friends are what make life most enjoyable—they are, in fact, its real purpose. We only pass this way once and, to the extent we wish it, our family and friends are our legacy—the interactions we have with others become the remembrances of those who come after. The first of the essays is "The Circle of Life," a cycle I could see at a beach club in New Jersey that my wife's family has been going to for about a hundred years. Our grandchildren are the fifth generation to use the same bathhouse. I marvel at what the walls have seen and heard, and am glad they cannot speak. The last essay is about my misspent school days, an experience from which my wife (before she was my wife!) ultimately rescued me, which shows the value of luck in our relationships and in our lives.

The Cycle of Life
August 14, 2006

Life is too important a thing ever to talk seriously about.

Lady Windermere's Fan, 1892
Oscar Wilde (1854–1900)

THE CYCLE OF LIFE SEEMS NEVER SO PRESENT as it does at the beach club to which we belong on New Jersey's north coast. Our grandchildren are the fifth generation—through my wife's side—to play in the baby pool, build sandcastles, and participate in the race between devouring an ice cream cone and losing it to the summer sun. And they do this as they crawl or stagger down the same boardwalk along which their great-great-grandparents staggered, perhaps under the influence of an unwise midday gin and tonic, a hundred years ago.

Within a few short months of giving birth, young mothers wheel their newborns toward the baby pool, which is no more than a slight indentation in the boardwalk conveniently situated next to the children's snack bar. The pool, approximately fifteen feet square, is about six inches deep at the shallow end. The water—polluted by the presence of dozens of diapered children throughout any given day, yet populated with healthy-looking children—is proof of the concept that immunity is the best prevention against disease. It is here that the cycle begins. On the table next to my bed is a picture of my wife, aged about three, looking at the camera with the water in the baby pool lapping at her ankles. Similar photos of my children exist, as do pictures, now, of most of my grandchildren, all in like attire and pose.

Next comes the migration to the beach—the draw being the hypnotic enticement of the waves—the opportunity for young, housebound mothers ("yummy-mummies," as a friend used to call them forty years ago) to work on their tans. Besides, it is the perfect venue for the building of sandcastles. (Despite the twice-daily tidal erosion, there is in these structures a greater sense of permanence than in the "starter castles" that populate New York's suburbs.) While their fathers huddle under spreading umbrellas, clutching the *New York Times* and avoiding the sun's rays, the slightly older children, now social animals, begin to form packs and race up and down the beach, daring the waves as they charge in and out. This is the time of endless summers. At the age of eight, a three-month summer vacation represents 3 percent of the child's entire young life. A like percentage of my life would be more than two years. Even though at my age I am far more conscious of the terminus of all good things, that still seems a long time.

Eventually, conscious of the need to improve swimming skills, many youths head to the big pool for lessons and a spot on the swim team. Competition begins at the age of five and continues through high school. My wife and my children have trophies attesting to varied individual aquatic skills. The beach is by no means abandoned, and certainly the teenagers, like those the world over, consider a nicely tanned body a social necessity. Lunch, if and when it is consumed by these young teens, is eaten farther up the boardwalk away from inquiring parental eyes. Their movements, however, are noted by us older observers.

Once the young are college-bound, summer finds them back at the club on weekends—a refuge from the poorly paid internships they endure in order that they may, in the future, participate in the American Dream. ID cards in hand, they head to the bar. Lunch is accompanied by a beer, a wine spritzer, or a rum Southside. Here they perch (when not back on the beach) for many visits over a period of years, which include those as young singles and as newlyweds.

For the older parents (those of us who will soon become grandparents), these years represent the calm before the storm, because we know that anon the cries of the newborn will signal the start of the next cycle—the trek back to the baby pool, the club's fountain of youth—bringing a new understanding to those last words from vespers: ". . . as it was in the beginning, is now, and ever shall be. . . ."

Family Get-Togethers
July 9, 2007

Ships that pass in the night, and speak each other in passing,
Only a signal shown and a distant voice in the darkness;
So on the ocean of life we pass and speak one another,
Only a look and a voice, then darkness again and a silence.

"The Theologian's Tale," 1863
Henry Wadsworth Longfellow (1807–1882)

A S HAS BEEN SAID HUNDREDS OF TIMES, people do not choose their families. The extent to which one maintains connections is a matter of personal choice. Time management suggests the increase in one's own family (children and grandchildren) necessitates a corresponding decrease in available time for other family members (siblings, cousins, etc.). That said, two events over the past Fourth of July week involved my broader family: the first, a sister's wedding, and the second, a family baseball game, now in its 119th year.

Longfellow's Wayside Inn in Sudbury, Massachusetts, was the site of the wedding on Saturday, June 30. Later, crossing the Longfellow Bridge to Cambridge in order to board the *Henry Longfellow* for a dinner tour of Boston Harbor, one could be forgiven for thinking Mr. Longfellow was the man of the hour. In fact, he was not. The couple consisted of my sister Charlotte and the man who became her husband, Fred Neinas.

The ceremony was simple and gracious, reverent and endearing, and was performed by a gentlemanly justice of the peace in the garden of the Wayside Inn with Henry Wadsworth Longfellow bearing witness in the form of a bas-relief in the garden wall. He gazed upon a congregation composed of Charlotte's and Fred's children and grandchildren along with siblings plus spouses. The wedding party consisted of Charlotte's daughter, Liz, as matron of honor and Fred's brother,

Leslie, as best man. The three eldest granddaughters were flower girls. A guitarist sang gently but effectively off to the side. The weather was perfect. Lunch followed at the inn and then, a few hours later, the dinner tour of Boston Harbor. Exiting the lock separating the Charles River from the harbor, the first visible sight is the USS *Constitution* made famous as "Old Ironsides" by Oliver Wendell Holmes. Fortunately for those of us alive today, fate did not heed Mr. Holmes when he wrote:

> *Oh, better that her shattered hulk*
> *Should sink beneath the wave;*
>
> *
>
> *And give her to the god of storms,*
> *The lightning and the gale!*

There she was, proud and tall, and to this day annually proves her seaworthiness via a very short sail. Our voyage continued through the harbor, past the steeple of the Old North Church (also made famous by Longfellow) and the renovated old wharves of the North End, now converted to attractive harbor-facing homes and office buildings—old and new living in harmony. The setting sun silhouetted Boston's skyline. Both the good and the evil of the modern world were visible in planes taking off and landing at Logan Airport and in police tape surrounding an aircraft carrier. Drinks and dinner provided a wonderful opportunity to catch up with my brothers and sisters, one or two of whom I had not seen for a couple of years.

◦

Four days later my wife and I found ourselves heading back to Massachusetts, along with our son Sydney and his family. Our destination: Wellesley, where since 1889 my paternal grandmother's side of the family has celebrated the Fourth of July with a baseball game and lunch. The entry in my great-great-grandfather's diary for July 4, 1889 reads simply, "Children and grandchildren played baseball." How surprised but pleased he would be to know that a tradition begun 118 years ago persists to this day. My grandchildren represent the seventh generation to be in attendance.

This year had special meaning for me. My grandfather, after whom I am named, was married in 1907, so this was the hundredth anniversary of his first attendance. We arrived about 11:00 a.m. The ball game was underway. While my son signed in and went onto the field, I opted to visit with relatives. An eighty-six-year-old second cousin once removed told me tales of playing with my father, who was ten years her senior. She also recalled a wonderful story from 1927, when she was six and received a pony. The pony stumbled exiting the trailer and appeared to "kiss" the ground, so she named it Charles Lindbergh after the aviator who a few weeks earlier had landed at Le Bourget Field in Paris and did kiss the ground upon his safe arrival. As usual the game ended about 12:30 p.m. and, as usual, in a tie. Lunch and the opportunity for a swim followed at another cousin's farm in South Natick, where George, my two-year-old grandson, learned the hazards of electric fencing. However, no harm was done, and by three o'clock we were headed back to Connecticut.

Each of us has our time to be a child, to be young, to mature, and to grow old. That continuum is visible in the figures and faces of relatives, some of whom I have known all my life, others of whom I just met. Fate, or the happenstance of fertility, determined my family, and I am thankful for the hand I was dealt. Following a week such as this, I am reassured that while we may be like ships that "pass in the night," family, continuity, and the warmth of belonging are of immeasurable value.

Thanksgiving 2007
November 26, 2007

The year that is drawing toward its close has been filled with the blessings of fruitfulfields and healthful skies. To these bounties, which are so constantly enjoyed that weare prone to forget the source from which they come, others have been added whichare of so extraordinary a nature that they cannot fail to penetrate and soften even theheart which is habitually insensible to the ever-watchful providence of Almighty God.

Abraham Lincoln
Thanksgiving Proclamation, October 3, 1863

THANKSGIVING IS TRULY A UNIQUE American holiday. It stems from the days of the Pilgrims in Plymouth Plantation, who in 1621 thanked God for their safe passage across three thousand miles of open water, for the abundance of their first harvest, but most importantly for the ability to worship as they pleased. From George Washington on, most of the early presidents (a notable exception being Thomas Jefferson) designated a national thanksgiving holiday. In 1863, President Lincoln declared Thanksgiving a federal holiday, a "prayerful day of thanksgiving," to take place on the last Thursday in November. President Franklin Roosevelt in 1939 set the date we celebrate today—the fourth Thursday in November.

This year we celebrated Thanksgiving in the newly decorated dining room of our daughter, Linie, at her home in Rye, New York, where she lives with her husband, Bill Featherston, and their three children: Caroline, age seven; Jack, who is five; and Henry, three. In the Northeast the weather was almost springlike; so my wife and I took the children—in anticipation of a hearty Thanksgiving meal—for a long walk to Jack's school, the Midland School. There the children played on swings, climbed a "rock" wall, and slid down slides, burning calories and expending energy. Back at her house, Linie was preparing for the meal.

Our daughter is gifted with an imagination and a color sense that permits boldness in decoration. Her house shows it, particularly the dining room, which she had painted a rich chocolate brown enhanced by a gold fabric wallpaper. The table was set with china, silver, and crystal. The result was stunning. Linie also has a Tom Sawyer–like ability to get others to help. Her mother made the dessert; her sister-in-law provided the vegetables and the starch; I cooked the turkey. Linie supervised.

Our oldest son, Sydney, was there with his wife, Beatriz, and their three young children. Despite the opportunity for chaos, we made it through the meal, fortified with good wine and stimulating conversation. The children generally stayed at their own table, and by the end of the day only one trip had been made to the emergency room—my granddaughter Caroline bruised her foot while in pursuit through the living room. However, she returned home after a couple of hours wearing an Ace bandage and a smile and carrying a little furry toy dog, provided by the hospital in lieu of a purple heart.

As a family holiday, Thanksgiving causes one to reflect on earlier celebrations. Dozens of memories glide through my mind, but four stand out. I have a photograph of our dining room table in Peterborough, New Hampshire, in 1955. My father is seated, poised with a carving knife and fork in midair, a big smile spread across his face. Around the circular table are eight of his nine children, all with a lean and hungry look on their reasonably clean faces. George, at two months, is napping. My mother is the photographer.

Thirteen years later my wife and I, along with two little children, attempted the drive to Peterborough, but were turned back by a snowstorm. Thanksgiving that year consisted of deli sandwiches. The following weekend we did drive up, and Monday my father died after a long bout with cancer.

In 1978, the family of my paternal grandparents gathered for Thanksgiving. Though my grandparents were both dead, their house in Wellesley was still in the family, belonging to an aunt. Fifty-four of us showed up. Name tags were issued, as there were cousins and spouses, some of whom had never met. Two of the guests came out of institutions for lunch. One had to return before dessert. The table, which sat forty-eight, consisted of tablecloth-covered plywood placed on sawhorses set up in the front hall. Six young girls dined off a table on the staircase landing. Everybody had been asked to supply a dish. Miraculously, it worked wonderfully. Whoever was in charge could have run a US Army regimental commissary.

Ten years later, I recall a snowy Thanksgiving in Greenwich, when among our guests were a Deerfield classmate of our son Edward, a young man named D. J. Kim from South Korea, and a Scotsman named Bob MacDonald with whom I then worked. Whenever I see Bob now, he reminds me of the human warmth that exuded from that family dinner and the subsequent walk along snow-filled roads, and how good he felt to be included.

Lincoln, during those dark days in the midst of a civil war, was able to find solace for which he gave thanks. Despite the slaughter on the battlefield—six hundred thousand lives would be lost during those four years—the population expanded during the 1860s by 10 percent—three million people. Lincoln's words then inspire us today. While the problems President Bush faces pale in comparison to those that confronted President Lincoln, each generation is presented unique challenges. As a nation we struggle with conflicting views as to the most efficient conduct of a war against Islamic terrorism while maintaining our sense of democratic values, and we debate how best to handle the fallout from the housing bubble and the myriad schemes (some fraudulent) used to finance that bubble. Amidst such turmoil, it is easy to lose sight of how much there is for which we all in this country should be thankful. There is great satisfaction to be gained from realizing that we live in a place deemed part of the New World, yet we function under the world's oldest democratic constitution. We give thanks for the fortune that permits us to be living at this time in this freest of all nations.

Catalogues
November 18, 2009

Satisfaction guaranteed or your money back.

Sears Roebuck catalogue banner in 1927

S UNDAY MORNING FOUND ME IN BED with four blondes. Before anyone gets the wrong idea, one was my wife and the other three were granddaughters, aged three (Sarah), six (Margaret), and seven, soon to be eight (Emma). We were staying in Darien with our son Edward and his wife, Melissa.

About seven, the girls will knock on the wall separating their room from ours. A return knock is an invitation to join us in bed. We talk. We read. This past Sunday I read a couple of "Froggy" books, *Froggy Plays in the Band* and *Froggy Gets Dressed*. And then the girls turned to the American Girl catalogue, a hoped-for source of Christmas presents. American Girl has been a retail sensation. The business was founded in 1986 by Pleasant Rowland, as the Pleasant Company. She was looking for dolls for her nieces (ages eight to twelve). In 1998 the business was sold to Mattel for $700 million and the name was changed to American Girl.

As the girls perused the catalogue and chatted with their grandmother about their Christmas wishes, I lay back on the pillows, my eyes shut, their voices becoming a distant murmur; I found myself remembering the catalogues my family received when I was a child in the late 1940s.

In the years immediately following World War II, the country remained divided between urban and rural dwellers. The suburbs would be built up very shortly, but in 1946 almost half the population lived in rural communities. Immigration and mechanization of farming had caused urban centers to grow rapidly from about 1880 to the late 1920s. The Depression and then the war slowed the rate of change, but did nothing to alter its direction. In the postwar years (1950–1960), millions relocated to the newly developed suburbs.

But in the late 1940s in rural New Hampshire, life was still pretty much as it had been twenty years earlier. There were no malls, no shopping centers. Keene, with a population of twenty thousand, was the largest town in the area, but was twenty miles away, so was only visited on special occasions. A department store, Derby's, served the needs of most of Peterborough's inhabitants.

Glamour came from catalogues, particularly the one from Sears Roebuck. Mail order had become a big industry in the last years of the nineteenth century and the first half of the twentieth.

Aaron Montgomery Ward in Chicago sent out the first catalogue in 1872. Ward had arrived in Chicago from New Jersey just after the Civil War. He found a job with the dry-goods merchant Field, Palmer, and Leiter, which later became Marshall Field and Company. In 1872, at the age of twenty-eight, Ward started a catalogue business to service his rural clientele. By 1897 he was publishing a thousand-page catalogue and employed a thousand clerks. Richard Warren Sears was a railroad agent in North Redwood, Minnesota, in 1886. An unwanted shipment of watches, which he purchased and then resold to other agents, gave him the impetus to start a business—buying watches and selling them through mail-order catalogues. He moved to Chicago and in 1893 incorporated the business as Sears Roebuck and Company, with Alvah C. Roebuck as his business partner.

After the war, Sears Roebuck became predominant as a catalogue merchandiser. Montgomery Ward, in December 1944, had been seized by the federal government for refusing to comply with labor laws; its chairman, Sewell Avery, was carried from his office in his desk chair by National Guardsmen. "To hell with government," he allegedly called out as he was toted away. While the Montgomery Ward catalogue continued to be printed and distributed in the postwar years, the company lost ground to Sears Roebuck.

So it was the Sears catalogue that we looked forward to, especially the Christmas edition, which arrived around Thanksgiving. Almost anything could be bought through the catalogue—clothes, toys, tools, stoves, groceries, even ready-to-assemble houses. An estimated seventy thousand homes were sold in North America by means of Sears Roebuck catalogues between 1908 and 1940, including, allegedly, the one in which Richard Nixon was born in Yorba Linda, California.

But it was the Christmas catalogue that provided the opportunity to dream. The bright colors and the perfect-looking, spotless children playing in ideal living rooms with toy trains seemed a world away from our home, a farmhouse with no central heat and a woodstove in the kitchen, filled with children and animals. Whatever lust existed in our hearts was directed at the idealized lives of those depicted in those doctored photographs.

If the purpose of the Christmas catalogue was to entice children to heckle their parents, it worked in our household. We spent hours daydreaming over Erector sets, bicycles, baseball gloves, and Monopoly games, daring to believe that this Christmas a Lionel model train would magically appear under the tree. It never happened, but by Christmas afternoon we had moved on to new presents—christening a new pair of skis now strapped to our feet on the new snow in the fresh, cold December air, or engrossed in a new Hardy Boys mystery, sitting next to the warming fire.

☙

Then the bed squeaked as the girls bounced gaily, the American Girl catalogue at their feet, and I was aroused from my dreams of an earlier, simpler time as the pages of Sears' Christmas catalogue dissolved. I was back in Darien, in bed with my four blondes and happy to be there.

On the Birth of My Ninth Grandchild
June 5, 2006

The chief part of human happiness arises
from the consciousness of being beloved.

The Theory of Moral Sentiments, 1759
Adam Smith (1723–1790)

SARAH ANNE WILLIAMS WAS BORN to my son Edward and his wife, Melissa, last Wednesday, May 31. My wife and I now have nine grandchildren. The birth was unique, at least in the annals of my family, and will likely be the source of stories for years to come. However, Melissa and Sarah are doing well and that is what's important.

It took my parents one generation to produce nine children, while my wife and I took two generations to accomplish the same. In other words, it took Caroline and me forty-two years to complete what my parents produced in seventeen. If we were both stocks, my parents would be accorded the higher multiple, though I might be able to argue that since all of our grandchildren have been born in a space of less than six years, we have added to the overall population growth rate.

Nicholas Eberstadt of the American Enterprise Institute, discussing Russia's population decline, explains America as an exception in a Western world faced with declining birthrates. Eberstadt writes that in the United States there are "three differences with Europe and most other advanced countries: greater optimism, greater patriotism, and stronger religious values." I do not believe that my patriotism or religious values are out of the ordinary, but my wife and I have always looked upon life in an optimistic way. Certainly we have had to dodge the odd curveball that life tosses from time to time, but on balance we count ourselves among the fortunate, and there is nothing like a new grandchild to add an "amen" to that feeling.

The great thing about grandchildren is that they allow one to par-

ticipate in the future and, in a small but personal way, to perhaps have some influence. In the birth of Sarah I again sense the magnificence and mystery of life, and I am humbled and awed in knowing that she carries some of my DNA. However, birth by its very nature gives rise to darker thoughts of mortality. As my gray head bends over this tiny child, I inhale her newborn-baby scent and I know that I will likely never see her as a mother and certainly never as a grandmother. She will be for me, like all my grandchildren, perpetually young. Every mother, at some point and at some level of consciousness, realizes that her most important job is preparing her child for independence. We see this in nature: the mare pushing her filly away; a robin urging its wing-empowered fledglings on their first flight; a swan nudging its baby cygnet into the water. A mother accomplishes this goal not only by providing food and shelter, but, as importantly, in the love she bestows, which breeds confidence, character, and understanding. So one generation passes on to the next.

The Wall Street Journal, in its lead editorial on June 2, wrote about Philip Longman's book *The Empty Cradle*, published in 2004. Longman takes to task the myth that population growth is a threat to our world and the environment. Many countries, both rich and poor, both in the West and the East, are experiencing serious population declines. The United States remains an exception, and as the *Journal's* editor wrote, "Our thriving economy is testimony to the fact that human beings, so long demonized as the ultimate threat to the planet, are its most indispensable resource." So for Caroline and myself, not only do we feel that we and our children are doing our part for mankind, but more importantly we exult in the delight and the joy of watching yet another grandchild begin her trip through life.

Dakota

June 1, 1987 – January 30, 2004

February 7, 2004

If there are no dogs in heaven,
then when I die I want to go where they went.

Will Rogers (1879–1935)

Dakota died Friday morning, January 30, at the age of sixteen years and eight months. She died as she had lived, with dignity. Cody, as she was known, had spent the night with our friends and neighbors Lennie and Jodi. She arose at 5:00 a.m. as Lennie began his day, asked for a biscuit as was her custom, and lay down for a quick nap before the day began in earnest. At some point, apparently in the next few minutes, she had a massive stroke and was unable to rise. Her embarrassment at the situation was compounded by her inability to control her bodily functions. Lennie knelt, reassured her, and cleaned her off.

Jodi telephoned first the vet, and then Caroline, who was home with our daughter, Linie, and her two children, the youngest of whom, Jack, is allergic to dogs. Cody was confused and scared, but under the spell of Lennie's comforting words and petting, she calmed down and relaxed. When the vet's office opened at eight, Jodi, Lennie, and Dakota were at the door, along with Caroline, who met them there. A quick diagnosis confirmed that, in fact, she had suffered a stroke, and her vital signs indicated the likelihood of another imminently. The vet suggested that putting her to sleep would be the correct and humane decision. Caroline concurred. Cody sniffed Caroline, knew that she was in loving hands, and further relaxed, her tail wagging softly. She died in keeping with her character, gently and ladylike.

Dakota had had an idyllic life, despite a harrowing first few weeks. She was born on June 1, 1987, in New Hampshire and was acquired by Ian Paine, a fraternity brother of our son Sydney. On the return to Hanover with the new puppy, the car in which they were riding was in an accident. Ian, who was holding the puppy, was killed, and the young puppy was tossed through a window, damaging her left eye. After a short stay at the vet, she was brought back to live at their fraternity, Psi Upsilon. Social life at college was incompatible with her more sober and pacific nature, so during parties she would retreat to the quiet of upstairs. She was often taken for walks. At one point, during a snowstorm, she dashed onto the road and had one of her paws damaged under the wheels of a passing car. By March of the following year the decision was made to have her leave the cloisters of college, her education now complete, and to come and live with us in Greenwich.

Life in Greenwich, where she would live for the next five years, was comfortable. She smoothly and swiftly fit into our lives. Two acres enclosed by an invisible fence provided a good place to explore. An elderly chocolate Lab of ours, Bundle, taught her the rules governing dogs in our household. Long walks, complemented by a swim in the reservoir, generally satiated her wanderlust—though it is true that on rare occasions something beyond the fence would capture her attention, and, heedless of the shock she knew she would receive, she would dash through the invisible fence. Her curiosity satisfied, she would return to the driveway, but now, with her adrenaline dissipated, she would be unwilling to accept the shock of re-crossing the barrier.

In 1993, at the age of six, Dakota moved with us to Old Lyme, where she would spend the next ten and a half years. This was heaven on earth for a dog who was half Lab and half golden retriever. There were nine acres, a marsh filled with special and unique smells, and the Duck River in which to swim. It was also in Old Lyme that Dakota made her first and, in truth, only real dog friend, Nijill. At the time we arrived in Old Lyme, Lennie and Jodi were living in a cottage on the property. Around 1995 they acquired a German shepherd and christened her Nijill. Nijill was large, as is typical of the breed; so she was scary to those unaccustomed to her, but she had a calm nature. Additionally, she was well trained by Lennie, who is sort of a pied piper to the animal world. In a game of catch, the two would race toward a thrown ball; Dakota was quicker, but the injured eye hindered her vision, and the view of Nijill charging toward the tossed ball suggested to her that discretion was indeed the better part of valor, so Cody would move discreetly to the side as Nijill charged the ball and roll onto her back in submission. Shortly before Nijill's death, Lennie acquired Jake, and then, even later, Brock. While these male German shepherds treated Cody with respect and provided protection, they never became the real friend that Nijill had been.

When considering adjectives to describe Dakota, words such as *loving, loyal, caring,* and *sensitive* come to mind. And those words do describe her, particularly in relation to the humans whom she knew and who cared for her. (Any person coming in contact with this dog could not help but love her.)

She was also curious and adventurous. Many times she would return to the house, a not very pleasant odor emanating from her damp and ruffled coat, following a romp in the marsh or a chase in the small wood on an adjoining property. Dead fish, skunks, and other unthinkables were usually the source of this unpleasantness. She loved taking walks, and was good on a leash. The highlight of an afternoon excursion would be a swim and retrieving tennis balls or sticks in the Back River at the boat landing at the foot of Smith Neck Road. She loved the seasons. In the heat of the summer she would crawl into a cool space she had dug out under some hedges. In the winter she would race out into the cold and the snow and roll around, heedless of the frigid weather. She traveled. For several years she spent the month of August with us in Rumson, New Jersey, where we rented a house on the Navesink River. She loved visiting Deerfield, Massachusetts, where our son Edward was at school. Lennie and Jodi often took her on their periodic trips to New Hampshire. Once she visited New York City, but quickly came to the conclusion that she was a country girl.

She was without question happiest in Old Lyme. The marshes and fields offered opportunities to explore, while the wildlife—rabbits, squirrels, and deer—provided endless fascination. If there was one thing about Old Lyme with which she was not happy, it was the fence around the pool. However, that was but a small impediment in her overall sense of contentment.

Dakota had a unique sense of timing. She was born the day before Edward's birthday and she died the day before mine. She was a special dog. We miss her, and we will always remember her.

An Afternoon with Thomas the Train
November 13, 2006

There's something about the sound of a train
that's very romantic, nostalgic, and hopeful.

Paul Simon (1941–)

GATHERING NINE GRANDCHILDREN, all under the age of six and a half, along with their parents—our three children and their spouses—is no easy task. However, once a year Thomas the Tank Engine pulls into Essex Junction, and so provides the perfect venue. Such was the case this past weekend—the sixtieth anniversary of Thomas's appearance in book form.

Thomas, who today is as familiar to young boys as Madeline is to young girls—and dates from the same era—was the brainchild of the Reverend Wilbert Vere Awdry (1911–1997), an Anglican clergyman in Birmingham, England, from 1936 until he retired in 1965. In 1942 his young son, Christopher, contracted measles; to entertain him, the Reverend Awdry made up train stories. Three years later *The Three Railway Engines* was published, introducing Edward, Gordon, and Henry. In 1946 *Thomas the Tank Engine* was published—and a star was born. Thomas, as a small tank engine, was identifiable to young children, as he struggled to compete in a world of bigger engines. As a grandfather, I can attest that the love affair young children, particularly boys, have with Thomas and his friends continues to blossom sixty years after the character was introduced. When my young grandsons visit, Thomas dominates the TV screen. Toy versions of Thomas and his friends lie scattered on the floor and, in the evening, a Thomas book is often the reading material of choice.

Replicas of Thomas the Tank Engine, which was based on a steam engine from the Victorian era, are shunted around the United States and hitched to working engines, one of which is an old steam engine in Essex, Connecticut. So vigorous is demand for seats, reservations must to be made weeks in advance.

This past Saturday was unusually warm for November, with the temperature in the mid-sixties and the sky free of rain, but slightly overcast—a perfect Indian summer day. With everyone present, we boarded car No. 9 for the 2:15 p.m. out of Essex Junction. No. 9 was the passenger car directly in front of Thomas, and the first among us to board commandeered sufficient seats for our crowd. On the way north Thomas pushed the cars from the rear with an assist from an old steam engine at the front of the train. As the train slowly—and reasonably gently—chugged along, we passed road crossings with people waving from their halted cars. Snubbing our noses, we went by the Essex Taxi Company. We looked out upon fields and streams. We saw boats stored for the winter, and a giant turkey composed of colorful balloons.

With the exception of George, who at twenty-two months enjoyed racing up and down the aisle, and Sarah (aged five months), who preferred napping in her mother's arms, the children were captivated by the scenery and the adventure of riding a train that would have been more at home one hundred years ago than in today's electronic age. Caroline and I, of course, were captivated by the horde of grandchildren. Like children everywhere, the four girls, aged three to six, sat together, while the boys, aged two and a half to five, scattered among the adults. Forty-five minutes after leaving, we returned amidst cheering and thanks to Thomas. We reentered the depot to a waving crowd.

"And where will Thomas return to when he leaves Essex?" asked the conductor. "The Island of Sodor," responded the knowledgeable youngsters. So he will, and we will go back to our own home filled with love and joy in the miracle of grandchildren.

Moving and "Stuff"

February 23, 2012

What we call the beginning is often the end
And to make an end is to make a beginning.
The end is where we start from.

"Little Gidding," *Four Quartets*, 1942
T. S. Eliot (1888–1965)

Where does stuff go when it dies? Does it go to stuff heaven?
George Carlin Comedian and social critic(1937–2008)

BURIED BENEATH THE MISCELLANEA that are the contents of my bedside table were eight fingernail clippers. They symbolize my squirrellike nature, upsetting to those who lead more orderly lives, like my daughter, Linie, whose house in Rye is a temple to beauty and organization. It is a trait that I unfortunately inherited from some loony ancestor who never threw a bone away when it could be used to make soup, or a stirrup if it could be turned into a cup. Of course, amidst all the rubbish there were some interesting finds, like the sales slip for a pair of end tables bought on December 5, 1965, from Nathan Liverant of Colchester, Connecticut, for $300. My son Sydney has become their guardian. And then there was the uncashed check for $100 from my son Edward, dated 1987, found in the drawer under an antique shaving mirror. I suggested to Edward that he place the check in the back of his daughter's dresser, so that she might find it years from now.

Last Thursday we moved out of our 900-square-foot, one-bedroom apartment on Sixty-Fourth Street in New York, after seventeen years. Even if we had not moved, we should have pretended to have done so. The amount of stuff one accumulates over a few years is amazing. A thorough housecleaning is cathartic. Dust balls the size of small mice behind two bookcases and my grandfather's desk; debris an inch thick beneath radiators that I am sure predated our time in the apartment. But most of the accumulation was my own. Rain would bring another umbrella, to be dumped in the closet alongside its predecessors, until there were a dozen or more. Gloves seemed to appear on their own, as though immaculately conceived. Each coat (and there was an abundance of those) housed its own pair.

Besides the gloves and umbrellas, there were eighty-two ties, thirty-three belts, seven surge protectors, fifteen pairs of shoes—I become exhausted just thinking of all that stuff. Even my seven-year-old grandson, George, when he saw innumerable boxes in the library in Old Lyme, asked, "How much stuff do you have, Pop Pop?"

Packing up books (about seven hundred), paintings (forty hung on the walls), photos (innumerable), and papers (countless) is endlessly fascinating, as I kept coming across something I had forgotten. A project that should have taken a few hours consumed days. Instead of packing boxes, I found myself looking closely at pictures, leafing through albums and papers, and skimming through forgotten novels. But, as George intimated with his question, I have too much stuff. There are those who suggest that apartments and houses should periodically be emptied. But Caroline and I are both collectors; so I doubt that is a route we are likely to take, at least willingly. Nevertheless, I did feel good putting old or unused items outside for the janitor to remove, but wondering, as did George Carlin, where it would go. My stuff, I am sure, has little chance of going to heaven.

When the last box had been removed and the van finally loaded, Caroline and I walked through the two rooms, our footsteps echoing off the empty walls; we were reminded of the first time we saw the place in January 1995, and the excitement we felt at getting an apartment in New York (to go with our house in Old Lyme) after twenty-five years of living in Greenwich. Part of me was sad, as our departure marked the end of one era; but another part was pleased, and I looked toward the future. As T. S. Eliot wrote, "And to make an end is to make a beginning."

While most of the "stuff" ended up in Old Lyme, the furniture is now in the homes of our children, where we can see it as often as we (and they) choose. So the end is not really even an end. I will continue to write "Thought of the Day" and the more sporadic "Notes from Old Lyme," and I will be in New York at least a few days every week, though now residing at the University Club, where I don't have to worry about my supper or making my bed. Their library exceeds anything I could imagine, and when I walk out of my room I simply shut the door.

But my home will be Old Lyme, a beautiful New England village where our house overlooks the marsh and the tidal flats of the Connecticut River as it empties into Long Island Sound. This is where Caroline has spent most of the last seventeen years. "Absence makes the heart grow fonder," as the old adage says; but when one reaches a certain age, flickers of mortality pass before half-dimmed eyes, and there appears less wisdom in that saying. I would rather think of Mr. Eliot's concluding lines: "The end is where we start from."

Reunion: Fifty-Five Years and Counting

June 13, 2014

Every parting gives a foretaste of death,
every reunion a hint of the Resurrection.

Arthur Schopenhauer (1788–1860)

ON THE SEVENTH OF JUNE, Caroline and I drove to Easthampton, Massachusetts, for the fifty-fifth anniversary of my high school graduation. Five days later, she looked at an e-mailed composite photograph of the eleven of us who attended. "Oh, my God," she blurted out, "they're so old!" It's true. We are. It wasn't staged—that is, Caroline's comment was not staged. The photograph was obviously staged, with, for example, my photo dropped in by master Photoshopper Andy Solomon, our class agent and an extraordinary photographer. Caroline's reaction was simply that of someone looking at eleven faces frozen in time; faces that could well have been framed and deposited in the attic of Dorian Gray's home. Or even faces of escapees from some nursing home for aged schoolboys, forlornly trying to recapture their youth.

Saturday turned out to be a beautiful day, as we drove the hour and a half from Old Lyme, Connecticut, to Williston Academy. It's easy: just follow the Connecticut River upstream until you reach Holyoke, then head west across Mount Tom and into Easthampton. The town itself is an old mill town, of which New England has hundreds. It is located about four miles south of Northampton, home of Smith College and former home of Calvin Coolidge, one of America's best and most underappreciated presidents.

We arrived shortly before lunch, and while we were waiting for some of my classmates to show, we struck up a conversation with a man who seemed about my age, except he was wearing (as we all were) a name tag with his senior-year photograph, indicating the class year '44, whereas mine said '59. His name was Bill Armstrong; though he now lives reasonably close, he had not been back for several years. He was the only one of his class to make it back for his seventieth; so we asked if he would like to become an honorary member of our class—at least for lunch. He quickly agreed. Given his year of graduation, I asked him about the war. It turned out that in December of his senior year, he'd joined the Army Air Forces, and was the only one in his class to graduate in uniform.

Bill was a spring chicken compared to John Williams, a cousin of my classmate Charlie DeRose, and a member of the class of '39. He was the only one of his class for their seventy-fifth. Besides being interesting, both men were delightful lunch companions. More importantly, they served to make us feel young and take the edge off what Caroline had later so despairingly (but accurately) described.

Others from my class who attended, besides Andy, Charlie, and me, were Fred Allardyce (now the school's chairman of the board of trustees), John Curtis, Phil Fisher, John Harper (a former roommate), Dave Raymond, Brewster Staples, Bob Stilson, and Roy Weiner. I missed Fred and Brewster, as they'd been there only for dinner the night before.

It is fascinating how one's character changes—becomes more juvenile, is the way my bride would describe it—as one retraces the steps and haunts of one's youth. Many of Williston's buildings are new, and some of those that have lasted this last half century have been remodeled almost beyond recognition. Remembrances of what had been rushed through my memory—a cemetery where I smoked cigarettes illegally, fields on which we once played, and a wood-paneled room in the field house where teas were held following sporting events. I remember once, after a junior varsity football game, being asked by a member of the opposing team, St. Paul's School, "What is Williston?" I told him it was a reform school, but not one for those who had committed capital crimes. He looked a little rattled, then walked away with one hand on his watch and the other clutching his wallet.

I knew, of course, about St. Paul's through friends and cousins.

My grandparents, my father's parents, had entered me in the Groton School when I was born. It was expected that I would enter the first form (seventh grade) in the fall of 1952. But when the time came, my parents demurred. The world had changed since their youth. Ten years of depression and five of war had greatly altered the world in which they had been brought up. For one thing, it had become more egalitarian. For another, my parents had brought us up by themselves, whereas they had been raised with nursemaids. They didn't want me out of the nest so young and so soon. So I stayed home, and any scholarly discipline I might have had went into hibernation, not to reemerge until two and a half years after graduation from Williston when I met the woman who became my wife.

By the time I entered high school, my parents must have been wondering if they had made a mistake in rejecting Groton. A great-grandfather, my mother's grandfather, had attended Williston in the 1850s, but their family had lost all connection. In desperation for a school, they turned to an old friend of my mother's family, Judge Thomas Swan of New Haven, who had been a Williston student in the 1890s and later served as chairman of their board of trustees. In a decision that he must have long regretted, he saw to it that I entered in the fall of 1956. The truth is I was immature and too much of a smart aleck, and, with minimal exceptions, never took advantage of what the school offered.

It wasn't, as I wrote earlier, until I met Caroline and my whole attitude changed that I began to realize what I had missed. About six months after we met, in the late spring of 1962 and shortly before I headed for Fort Dix as an army recruit, Caroline and I drove from Boston to Easthampton to have dinner with headmaster Phillips Stevens and his lovely wife, Sarah, who today, at age ninety-five, lives in our part of Connecticut. It was good for me to see the school in that context, having grown more serious as my love for Caroline deepened.

Now, fifty-two years after that dinner in the Homestead, we returned to the same building to register for the reunion. It was good fun to see some of those with whom I had spent so many impression-able years: to remember who we had been, but also to see who we had become. The visible passage of time, so obvious in a reunion of this sort, makes one realize how short is our time on this earth and how important it is to savor each moment. In life, as the philosopher said, it is the trip that is important, not the destination.

As we wandered around the campus before and after lunch, and as we visited with old friends, some of these thoughts came to mind—thoughts of what had been, of what might have been, but, most impor-tant, what was and what is. While neither my experience at Williston as a student nor Caroline's years at Westover had been the best, they taught us to make sure we would do whatever it took to ensure that our children had positive school experiences. We did, and they did.

The Death of a Friend

October 25, 2011

So when a great man dies,
For years beyond our ken,
The light he leaves behind him lies
Upon the paths of men.

"Charles Sumner," 1875
Henry Wadsworth Longfellow (1807–1882)

O UR FIRM LOST A GOOD FRIEND when Fred Stein died suddenly Sunday evening. He was just shy of his eighty-fifth birthday.
Fred's greatest success was the collecting of friends; he was a "people
person." Along the way he also amassed considerable wealth. In the
world of finance, he was a giant, and he knew and was known, loved,
and respected by thousands of all ages.

His death causes us to pause and reflect on our own mortality, on
the importance of family and friends, and to consider: by what legacy
will we be remembered?

So busy are we in our daily lives with our concerns for the immediate future that we rarely (and fortunately) do not think that life will
end one day—fortunately in the sense that if we were to pass our lives
in reflection, nothing would ever get done. His death makes us realize
the value of time. It makes clear that each moment that passes is one
that has disappeared forever.

Retrospection, in small doses, is healthy. Death is a natural and inevitable consequence of life. Shakespeare wrote: "All that lives must die
/ Passing through nature to eternity." A giant sequoia might live more
than half a millennium; an insect, perhaps a day or less. According
to Joel Cohen, a mathematical biologist at Rockefeller University, the
global average age for man is seventy. By that measure, Fred lived a full
life. But death always arrives too early. On learning of a friend's death,

our minds immediately turn to words unspoken, to deeds undone. It serves as a reminder to do the things we want to do, and to speak and be with those we cherish.

The greatest gift of life is a sense of wonder and curiosity—traits natural to children and too often sloughed off by adults. Those gifts presuppose a belief in the future. Fred embodied that attitude. It was what drew him to young people. It was what made him so knowledgeable about fields as diverse as art, literature, opera, and the financial markets. Instinctively or knowingly, Fred recognized that life is a continuum, with no knowable beginning and no knowable end. He knew that the value the elderly bring to the young is not so much wisdom as a link to the past—a past they otherwise know only through books. And the value the young bring to those of us who are older is a glimpse into the future—a future we will never see.

At the risk of being overly sentimental, Fred's death is a reminder that there is nothing so valuable as family and friendships; those relationships should be nurtured, so that the rewards they provide can be shared and enjoyed.

Above all else, we should remember Fred for his friendship, for his wisdom, and for the curiosity that kept him forever young. He enriched our lives and we are all better for having known him.

Letter to Vail Skiing Friends
December 10, 2002

Dear_____

As summer becomes but a memory and the first tinge of frost on a cool October day gives promise of winter, I woke to the realization that soon I would be skiing and, especially, skiing in Vail with good friends.

Friendship is a peculiar state. Real friends don't need constancy. True friendship involves respect, empathy, and shared interests. True friends can stand the test of time. It is fascinating to consider how we share this week—how we laugh with one another, how intimate we are—but when the bell tolls for the last run we go our separate ways, only to reappear the next year; and when we meet again, it is as though we had seen each other the previous day.

I write each of you because I treasure your friendship. In my business, we tell our salespeople that the key to success is relationships. Make the customer a friend. No amount of technology or fancy telecom equipment can replace a personal visit. And so it is in life. When the race has been run and the score is being tabulated, it is neither the weight of one's purse nor the size of one's house that will determine one's placement; it is, rather, the friends we have made, the smiles we have generated, the hearts we have warmed.

So next fall, when the leaves begin to turn and memories of languid summer days begin to fade and I find myself checking my ski equipment, it will be not only in anticipation of feeling the snow glide beneath my skis, but it also in the realization that I will soon again be with good friends who, physically, have been absent for a year. For a week we will live almost exclusively in one another's company where we will store such good memories as to sustain us for another year.

Love,
Sydney

A Fiftieth Anniversary
April 11, 2014

Love is composed of a single soul inhabiting two bodies.

Aristotle (384–322 BCE)

I NEVER DIVED TO THE BOTTOM OF THE OCEAN, nor have I ever ascended Everest. I never ran a marathon, nor did I (or will I) make a billion bucks. I never sang at the Met, nor did I ever ski the Matterhorn. But together, Caroline and I made it through fifty years of marriage—a feat more daunting than those listed, and certainly one more cherished.

Neither my parents nor hers made it to fifty years of marriage. Death intervened. Of our four sets of grandparents, only one made it to fifty years, my paternal grandparents. Ironically, they were the oldest of that batch to marry, both being in their thirties, something unusual when they were married in 1907. There was a small family party for them in 1957 in Wellesley, which was good fun. But they seemed pretty old to me at the time. Consequently, I do my best to act young and be as vigorous as possible when around my own grandchildren!

It doesn't seem that long ago that I was standing at the altar in the chapel of the Church of the Heavenly Rest on New York's Fifth Avenue. My brother Frank was at my side, as were two cousins and Caroline's brother. My sister Betsy and the wife of Caroline's cousin were her attendants. The rector, Floyd Thomas, stood behind us. I was twenty-three and nervous. And then Caroline Elliott appeared coming down the aisle—a vision of beauty—on her reluctant father's arm. And why wouldn't he be reluctant? He was seventy-one years old, a Princeton and Harvard Law School graduate. I was a boy from New Hampshire with a year to go in college—the University of New Hampshire—from which I had dropped out for a couple of years to work and to go into the army. I was not what one would have called a promising prospect. On the other hand, I have been blest with an innate sense of optimism. I am one who prefers "what might be" to "what could have been."

The first lines of Edgar Albert Guest's poem "It Couldn't Be Done" come to mind:

> Somebody said that it couldn't be done
> But he with a chuckle replied
> That "maybe it couldn't," but he would be one
> Who wouldn't say so till he tried.

(It would be a mistake, though, to overplay the country-boy rube bit, as my father, his father, and both his grandfathers were Harvard men, while most of the males in my mother's family had gone to Yale. One exception was my favorite uncle, who went to Trinity. I was simply a lad late to mature.)

In many respects, Caroline and I had an ideal start. Being young and in college meant we had low overhead and no expectations about material goods. There was no peer pressure. We grew into our new married state. We both worked: Caroline typing a manuscript, with me balancing three jobs and my courses. Between classes I drove a school bus, worked in a sandwich shop, and wrote a sports column for *Foster's Daily Democrat*. Ten months after we were married, in February, I had completed my degree and had a job lined up with the Recordak division of Eastman Kodak beginning in June. So we took $2,000 we had saved (our rent was $85 a month and we allocated $10 a week for groceries), bought two round-trip tickets to Paris, booked rooms for the night we arrived and the night before we were to leave, and hired a Volkswagen Beetle. For the next eleven weeks, with Arthur Frommer's *Europe on $5 a Day* tucked in our bag, we drove where impulse took us—France, Spain, Italy, Austria, Germany, Switzerland, and back to France. It was a time to unwind, a time to really know one another, and an opportunity to prepare for the grown-up world we faced on our return.

In 1971, we ended up in Greenwich, with our third child only a few days old. It was where we would live for the next twenty-four years. (In the interim, I had left Kodak and joined Merrill Lynch in New Haven.) In New York I went to work for the predecessor firm of Monness, Crespi, Hardt, and Company, the firm to which I returned in 1992 after an absence of seventeen years. Greenwich was where our children grew up and where we made many of the friends we still have today. In 1993, we moved into the house in Old Lyme, which we had bought a couple of years earlier and renovated, and where we live today.

When asked about the secret of staying married for fifty years (or just surviving that long), my response is that there is no secret, except that by marrying young you increase the probabilities. A successful marriage obviously requires love for the other person, but it also combines a willingness to share, to be empathetic and supportive, and to accept that things will not always be just as one wants. As much as anything, a successful marriage depends on luck. How well can one know someone after a year or so of dating? How can one tell if one will be a good mother or father? There is much that is left to chance, but like most successful endeavors marriage also takes work, a willingness to listen, and the acceptance that each is an individual. In many respects Caroline and I are very different, yet she is my best friend. There is no one with whom I would rather have dinner or spend the weekend.

We know we have been lucky. In a world marked by uncertainty, I am grateful for the sense of permanence we have been afforded. And my sense is that the permanence of our relationship has been good for our children.

We will be celebrating by renewing our wedding vows this afternoon, something our grandchildren have encouraged. Richard van Wely, who for many years was rector at St. Barnabas Church in Greenwich, will officiate. Caroline will have as her attendants our six granddaughters, ranging in age from five to thirteen. I will be accompanied by our four grandsons, the youngest being nine and the oldest thirteen. The congregation will consist of our children and their spouses, along with Richard's attractive wife, Judy. As I stand at the altar this time, I will not have the same fears that consumed me fifty years ago. I promise not to think of the word *altar* as described by Ambrose Bierce in *The Devil's Dictionary*: "The word is now seldom used except with reference to the sacrifice of their liberty by a male and female fool."

We will adjourn to the Belle Haven Club for a wedding supper, thanks to our son Sydney and his wife, the authoress Beatriz. Next week all eighteen of us will go to the Hillsboro Club in Florida for a few days over Easter weekend, where Caroline and I will prepare for our next fifty years. The last fifty have been like life in a playpen. I expect and hope the next fifty will be more of the same.

One Man's Education
December 29, 2014

You are always a student, never a master.
You have to keep moving forward.

Conrad Hall (1926–2003)
Cinematographer

THE END OF THE YEAR IS A GOOD TIME to reflect on subjects we deem of particular importance. Education, along with stability at home, is perhaps the most critical requirement for future success. I want to offer my own experience and to provide some additional thoughts. In public schools, administrators too often put students and parents second to the demands of unions. They are, for example, reluctant to approve options available to the well-off. Vouchers and charter schools are inimical to their interests. In colleges and universities, political correctness has driven out the concept of liberalness—the importance of confronting differing opinions. Walter Lippmann once wrote: "When genuine debate is lacking, freedom of speech does not work as it is meant to work." With ten grandchildren in school, education, especially its promises, is close to my heart.

Too often, our high schools are considered successful if 80 percent of their students graduate on time and matriculate. The fact that many seniors may be illiterate and/or innumerate seems of little concern. Any number of colleges and universities—for-profit as well as not-for-profit—have sprung up to accommodate the growing supply of students, most of whom must borrow the cost of tuition, and many of whom are unqualified. They have been told that a college degree—not education—is critical to success.

What has been lost in this mechanical process of sloppy manufacturing has been learning how to think. Too often, high school students graduate in need of remedial training. College seniors, in turn, graduate unprepared for the real world. I recognize that condemnation is broad; it ignores hundreds of good schools—public and private—and tens of thousands of even better teachers. But as a generalization it stands; for learning should be pleasurable, solid, and provocative.

I am sensitive to this issue because of my own experience. While I grew up in an educated household—my father, like his father and both his grandfathers, was an alumnus of Harvard—I never took advantage of the opportunities offered . . . or I did not until I was twenty-one, after I met the woman who became my wife. I blame only myself. I did have a few teachers in school and in college who tried to reach an unreachable boy. I remember those few fondly, and some of what they taught did stick, in spite of my best efforts to remain impervious to their attempts.

As a youngster, I liked to read. I loved Greek and Roman mythology, and read the Scribner classics. I read and enjoyed books of lesser importance, like the Hardy Boys series. By the age of fourteen, I had read Carl Sandburg's two-volume biography of Abraham Lincoln, and memorized the Gettysburg Address. About the same age, I became the youngest member of the high school debating team. But around that time I became rebellious; so when I went off to boarding school—Williston Academy in Easthampton, Massachusetts—I was in no mood to study, or to behave as I should.

After barely graduating, I scraped my way into the University of New Hampshire. I recall a professor of algebra handing back an exam, telling me it was the lowest mark he had ever given, but also noting that I had scored one of the highest marks ever recorded on the university's math entrance exam. After two years of dissipated living, I left. I worked, met Caroline, joined the army, and returned to college. When I had less than a year to go in college, Caroline and I married.

Looking back at those pre-Caroline years, I regret not having had a positive interaction with teachers and professors. But my mishaps provided lessons. First, my wife and I worked to ensure that our children would have positive school experiences, which they did. Second,

I established a personal reading curriculum. Generally, I read about thirty-five books a year, divided roughly equally between fiction and nonfiction. For the past fifteen years, I have maintained a record of the books I have read. I collect and read a fair amount of P. G. Wodehouse, and it is easy to forget which titles I've perused. Additionally, the list allows me to more easily recall what I have read and which books I enjoyed most. In terms of fiction, besides Wodehouse and my daughter-in-law Beatriz's novels, I prefer mysteries and classics, including Dickens, Anthony Trollope, Jane Austen, Edith Wharton, and Willa Cather. Character studies in great literature provide clues to human behavioral responses. Biographies and history help us understand the manifestations of that behavior.

Writing "Thought of the Day" requires staying abreast of current events. Most days I read six papers, as well as numerous publications and essays sent to me. While I am not a fan of the editorial page of the *New York Times*, it is like perusing enemy dispatches, as a friend put it. We should know what the other side thinks. One reason our country is polarized is that most people tend to read and watch only that which supports their beliefs. And college graduates tend to mimic what they have been taught in our "liberal" universities, institutions where open forums have become rare.

A baby is born with an empty brain, but with an insatiable appetite for learning. Watching my grandchildren grow from infancy to childhood to early teens, I have been amazed at how fast they learn and how rapacious is their desire. The role of a teacher is to keep inquisitiveness alive. The role of the school is to support teachers. There are few jobs more critical than that of the one charged with encouraging and channeling curiosity, in a bid to satisfy the quest for knowledge. As children get older, other interests intercede and distractions appear. Students must understand the consequences of decisions. Einstein said, "Education is . . . the training of the mind to think."

Learning is fun and exciting. That flame should never be doused. It is incumbent on all of us to continue our own education; to inspire our youth; to inculcate the desire to learn; to question; to think; to seek answers, even where none may be found. In spite of my criticism of our educational system and despite how poorly our students do in international competition, no other country comes close to ours in terms of creativity and innovation. Something is working.

It is telling that one of the more successful TV series is the Discovery Channel's *How It's Made.* Over the past dozen years, the Canadian company that created the show has documented the process behind 1,200 products, from pantyhose to race-car engines. Young people want to learn. School administrators could learn something from watching this program. Education should encourage aspiration and independent thinking. As we roll into 2015, our New Year's resolutions should include: don't stop learning and don't stop thinking! *Happy New Year!*

Another Birthday!
January 29, 2015

How old would you be if you didn't know how old you are?

Satchel Paige (1906–1982)

It takes a long time to become young.

Pablo Picasso (1881–1973)

IN TWO DAYS I TURN SEVENTY-FOUR. "My God," some will say. "I had no idea he was such a child. He seemed so old." Others will say, "The old goat really is old. He seemed so immature."

On commencing one's seventy-fifth year, one can be excused for thinking of mortality, but healthily, not morbidly. We know that everything alive will die; and we can be excused for feeling that this is not our time. There is a wisp of truth to the old saying "One is as old as one feels." Lewis Carroll had old Father William stand on his head and then, at the end of the poem, threaten the youth: "Be off, or I'll kick you down-stairs." In contrast, T. S. Eliot advised readers: "Be careful of Old Deuteronomy." There is wisdom in Satchel Paige's observation, quoted above: Does knowing our age influence who we are? Is my birth certificate accurate? I assume it is, but I have no memory of being born. Perhaps I will not be turning seventy-four? Do I care? No. It's as good a day as any.

Picasso had it right too: it does take a long time to become young. As children, we said whatever was on our minds. The same is true when we are older. Age provides freedoms, especially of expression, though perhaps less of the physical variety. We are less mindful (but hopefully still respectful) of what others think, so more apt to speak as we please. A few weeks ago in the *New York Times*, Anne Karpf, a British journalist and sociologist, wrote: "Our sense of what's important grows with age. We experience life more intensely than before, whatever our physical limitations, because we know it won't last forever"—a sobering but compelling thought.

A mid-seventies birthday is an opportunity to consider how differently various cultures treat the aged. The price of medicine translates into a high—some, like Dr. Ezekiel Emanuel, who feels that seventy-five is a good age to die, might say exorbitant—cost of keeping the elderly alive. Jared Diamond, UCLA professor and author of *Guns, Germs, and Steel* and who writes on the subject of aging, gave a lecture a few years ago: "Honor or Abandon: Why Does Treatment of the Elderly Vary So Widely Among Human Societies?" Japan celebrates Respect for the Aged Day. Other societies do not. Some of what he noted may have been true, but was a little creepy. Natural selection, he said, meant that there had been times and circumstances—starvation, for example, particularly among nomadic tribes—when it was deemed right for children to abandon or kill their parents. Not an outcome I particularly desire! But Professor Diamond's principal point was that Eastern cultures place greater value on family and the elderly than do Western ones, with the latter's tendency to celebrate youth and self-reliance. Improved medical care and better living standards mean that we are all living longer. As societies, we are aging, which will have consequences. Affordability will be one of them.

Not surprisingly, as it would give me but a year or so to live, I disagree with Dr. Emanuel. I suspect that if he enters his seventy-fifth year in good health, he might revise his opinions and perhaps decide that eighty or eighty-five might be a better age to call it quits. While I disagree with his concept of targeting a specific age, I do not want to live as a vegetable, or be so impaired I cannot perform the simplest tasks. I don't want to be carried by one of my sons, as Anchises was by Aeneas. But I would rather that any decision be made by my family, not the state.

Mental gymnastics are as important as their physical kin in holding back aging, but the process cannot be stopped. As an old southern expression has it: "Ain't time a wrecker!" It is, and despite the allegation by Ponce de León, there is no Fountain of Youth; there are only face-lifts, Botox, and the like, all of which are obvious to even the casual observer. The march of time is inexorable. Trying to stop the aging process is as futile as attempting to turn back the tide, as Canute discovered. So we are best off getting on with it and enjoying ourselves.

Those among us fortunate to have grandchildren derive an invaluable secondary benefit as we age. When we were new parents, our children looked upon us as the font of all knowledge. Soon enough, realism replaced credulity, as our fallibilities surfaced and became too obvious to ignore. With grandchildren, we get a second shot. These are sensations normally available only to those the media worships—Democratic presidents, movie stars, athletes, rock stars. However, like belief in Santa Claus or the tooth fairy, we know that this adulation too will pass. In the meantime, such adoration provides for wonderful moments of confidence building. While the limits to our knowledge will soon be exploited by our fast-learning grandchildren, there is, if I may be so bold, something more lasting in the wisdom we have accumulated and can offer. Professor Diamond concluded his lecture: "So, if you want to get advice on complicated problems, ask someone who is seventy; don't ask someone who is twenty-five."

Sitting at my computer, I note that I am sixteen years older than was my father when he died and only five years younger than my mother when she slipped her harness. But I emerge from that self-induced funk and look out at the snow accumulating in the fields, sense the cold of the ground underneath, but derive comfort from the knowledge that beneath that frozen soil lives the promise of spring and the resurrection of life.

The most important thing to realize, as birthdays appear with what seems increasing frequency, is how lucky we are to be here in the first place. When one considers the happenstance of our parents meeting, and their parents before them (going back thousands of generations), and the billions of spent sperm and unfertilized eggs that are wasted, the odds against any individual being born are billions and billions to one. So life must be rejoiced in, and part of life is getting older. We should not rue that fact. I do not feel as did T. S. Eliot's J. Alfred Pru-frock, though I admit to losing height:

> *I grow old . . . I grow old . . .*
> *I shall wear the bottoms of my trousers rolled.*

We should celebrate life, no matter our age. We are indeed lucky to be here, and I am even more fortunate to have a family I love, to be healthy, and to be having another birthday. I hope for many more.

Remembering 1965
April 20, 2015

Without memory, there is no culture.
Without memory, there would be no civilization, no society, no future.

Elie Wiesel (1928–)

Several years ago, while selecting a telephone number for our home in Old Lyme, my wife was unable to obtain 1964, the year we were married. She was also not able to get 1966, 1968, or 1971, the years our children were born. So she settled on 1965—the first full year of our marriage . . . and our last without children.

Our first wedding anniversary (April 11, 1965) was spent in Vienna. We had dinner that evening at Griechenbeisl, Vienna's oldest restaurant, dating back to the fifteenth century. About ten days ago, we had another Viennese weekend of sorts. Saturday we saw the movie *Woman in Gold,* a story of a woman living in Pasadena who, defying all odds, sues and wins back a portrait of her aunt (a painting considered the *Mona Lisa* of Austria). It had been stolen by the Nazis in 1939. The next day we saw Mona Golabek in her one-woman show *The Pianist of Willesden Lane* in Hartford. Both the movie and the show are based on actual events; both are worth seeing. The latter tells the story of Mona's mother, Lisa Jura, a musical prodigy who, at age fourteen in December 1938, was sent from Vienna to London. Her mother, whom she would never again see, said to her as she put her on the train: "Hold on to your music." She traveled via the Kindertransport, a rescue effort by which ten thousand Jewish children were saved over a nine-month period from almost certain death in Nazi prison camps. Lisa did, however, hang onto her music—and so has her daughter.

We began 1965 living in a small apartment in Durham, New Hampshire, with a bedroom so tiny that in order to get to the bathroom, one had to crawl across the bed. The year ended with us moving into a five-room Cape in Glastonbury, Connecticut. My new job paid $6,500, about the median for a household that year. The house cost $19,000, about $5,400 above the national average, according to the US Department of Commerce. (Accounting for some of the inequality we currently read about, median household income has increased eight-fold to $54,000 since then, while home prices have risen elevenfold to $220,000. Adding fuel to the inequity, stock prices, as measured by the Dow Jones Industrial Average, are up twenty times, while GDP is higher by twenty-three times.)

It was a year of protests that, while violent, had not reached the deadliness of the late 1960s and early 1970s. Civil rights and Vietnam were the primary causes. While President Lyndon Johnson had signed the Civil Rights Act of 1964 the previous July that declared segregation illegal, Jim Crow laws remained in effect throughout much of the South. Voting rights were the reason for Martin Luther King Jr.'s January speech at Brown Chapel in Selma, Alabama, a speech given in defiance of an anti-meeting injunction. Two months later, six hundred protesters marched east over the Edmund Pettus Bridge. Their goal: a peaceful protest at Alabama's capital in Montgomery. However, on the far side of the bridge, the marchers were attacked by state and local police with nightsticks and tear gas. That same year race riots broke out in other cities, notably in the Watts neighborhood of Los Angeles.

On the other side of the globe, the United States was becoming embroiled in what would become a twelve-year war in the jungles of Vietnam. The United States had been involved in Vietnam in a minor way since the defeat of the French in 1954 at Dien Bien Phu by Ho Chi Minh. But it was the White House–approved assassination of Vietnam's president, Ngo Dinh Diem, in 1963 that caused the die to be cast. It was not until February 1965, though, that America's participation in the war intensified, when Lyndon Johnson approved Operation Rolling Thunder. This was an aerial attack on Hanoi and Haiphong, which began in earnest in March and had the objectives of destroying the north's industrial and transportation base, halting the flow of men and material into the south, and raising the morale of the people in Saigon. It failed on all counts. In November, the Battle of la Drang Valley in South Vietnam's central highlands was the first major conflict involving US troops, a battle that saw American soldiers facing an enemy as committed and as idealistic as were they. It is a story movingly told by Lieutenant General Harold G. Moore and Joseph Galloway in *We Were Soldiers Once . . . And Young.* The outcome was unclear, but by the end of the year, there were 125,000 US troops in Vietnam. Antiwar protests intensified.

Back in the Northeast, those of us who lived through it will never forget the massive power blackout that occurred on November 9 and affected thirty million people. Oil was discovered in the UK portion of the North Sea. Rhodesia declared independence from Great Britain and became Zimbabwe. Malcolm X was shot and killed in New York City. In an act whose ramifications are still being felt today, the Higher Education Act of 1965, which provided low-interest loans for students, was enacted into law. Warren Buffett gained control of Berkshire Hathaway at $18 a share. (Today's price of $212,982 per share represents a compounded annual return of 20.6 percent!) The Beatles, who had first appeared on *The Ed Sullivan Show* the year before, were, with the Rolling Stones, the year's most popular musicians. Jerry Garcia and the Grateful Dead played their inaugural concert in San Francisco. *The Sound of Music* and *Goldfinger* were two of the top films. The Los Angeles Dodgers won the World Series, beating the Minnesota Twins in seven games. Lucky Debonair won the Kentucky Derby. And, hard to believe, Charles de Gaulle was then president of France.

As for my wife and me—I finished college in February. After lining up a job with Eastman Kodak, Caroline and I, with $2,000, took off for eleven weeks in Europe. We had no fixed plans other than hotel rooms booked in Paris for the night we arrived and the evening before we were to return home. With Arthur *Frommer's Europe on $5 a Day* and sleeping bags, we drove a rented VW bug throughout Europe. It was a delightful belated honeymoon that neither of us will ever forget. Back home, following a four-week training session with Kodak's Recordak division, I was assigned to the World's Fair for two months. We lived at my in-laws' apartment in New York, until I was transferred to an office in Hartford. There we rented a room in an old-fashioned boardinghouse for about a month, until we moved into our Cape. I was still in the US Army Reserve, but with traveling and moving, they didn't catch up with me until the next year.

Thinking of those days half a century ago brings to mind Tennessee Williams's observation: "Life is all memory, except for the one present moment that goes by you so quick you hardly catch it going." It is a message that resonates: when we allow each day to slip by unappreciated, we have no one to blame but ourselves.

ACKNOWLEDGMENTS

FIRST, I TAKE FULL RESPONSIBILITY for all errors in fact, as well as in grammar, spelling, and sentence structure.

I want to thank all who helped convert my random scribblings into coherent essays. Bauhan Publishing, which publishes some of New England's finest books, is run by the inestimable Sarah Bauhan. My thanks go to Sarah and her team, which includes Mary Ann Faughnan, editorial director; Henry James, art director; Kirsty Anderson, designer; and Jody Hetherington, editor. Mary Ann and Jody rendered my rough prose into readable English. Henry's artistic abilities brought the cover and interior illustrations to life, and Kirsty created the attractive design of the text.

While I have retired from my years on Wall Street, all of the essays were written while I was working at Monness, Crespi, Hardt and Company. Thus I want to thank Andy Monness, Neil Crespi, and Herb Hardt for their encouragement in my efforts.

Many of these essays touch on my extended family and on friends I have developed over the years. You know who you are, and I thank you from the bottom of my heart. As for Mitzi Perdue, P. J. O'Rourke, Brian Dennehey, Steve Hannah, and Dr. Theodore (Ted) Vanitallie (all of whom were kind enough to write blurbs for this book)—I will always be in your debt. Charles Gould's Preface makes me blush in embarassment; it is far more than I deserve. I want to extend special thanks in appreciation of my brother Willard who owns and manages The Toadstool in Peterborough, New Hampshire, named by BuzzFeed in its list of forty-four great American bookstores that everyone should visit.

Last, but far from least, I want to thank my immediate family: my children, Sydney, Linie, and Edward; their spouses, Beatriz, Bill, and Melissa; my ten grandchildren, Caroline, Alex, Emma, Jack, Anna, Margaret, Henry, George, Sarah, and Edith, and most important my wife Caroline, without whom none of this would have been possible, and to whom this book is dedicated. I love you all.